Figuring History

by

Lionel Gossman

AMERICAN PHILOSOPHICAL SOCIETY
Philadelphia • 2011

TRANSACTIONS of the
American Philosophical Society
Held at Philadelphia
for Promoting Useful Knowledge
Volume 101, Part 4

ISBN: 978-1-60618-014-3
US ISSN: 0065-9746

Library of Congress Cataloging-in-Publication Data

Gossman, Lionel.
 Figuring History / Lionel Gossman.
     p. cm. -- (Transactions of the American Philosophical Society held
at Philadelphia for promoting useful knowledge; v. 101, pt. 4)
 "With an online portfolio of 280 images."
 Includes bibliographical references.
 ISBN 978-1-60618-014-3
 1. Historiography--Methodology. 2. Historiography--Graphic methods. 3.
Historiography--Statistics. 4. Pictures as information resources. 5.
Visual communication--History. 6. History in art. 7.
History--Philosophy. 8. History--Study and teaching. 9. Illustration of
books--History. 10. Communication and culture--History. I. American
Philosophical Society. II. Title.
 D16.G675 2011
 907.2--dc23
                              2011045091

Cover illustrations:

Jean Froissart, *Chronicles*, Breslau Manuscript (1468), vol. 3, fol. 147, "John of Lancaster is greeted by the burghers of Bayonne." In Arthur Lindner, *Der Breslauer Froissart* (Berlin: Kommissions-Verlag von Meisenbach, Riffarth & Co., 1912), plate 3. Princeton University Library.

William Playfair, *An Inquiry into the Permanent Causes of the Decline and Fall of Powerful and Wealthy Nations* (London: Greenland and Norris, 1805), fold-out chart 4, facing p. 214. Orlando F. Weber Collection of Economic History. Rare Books Division. Department of Rare books and Special Collections. Princeton University Library. The same chart appeared as plate 19 in the 3rd edition of Playfair's *The Commercial and Political Atlas* (London: J. Wallis, 1801).

Author's Introductory Note

This essay began as an investigation into the use of graphs (flow charts, bar charts, and pie charts) as a means of conveying information about the past and even, especially in the case of the flow chart, of picturing a temporal development in a single still image—a feat that traditional representational images by their nature have been deemed unable to perform. Though common in antiquity and in medieval manuscript chronicles, images representing historical scenes and actions are in fact largely absent from the work of serious modern (seventeenth, eighteenth, and nineteenth-century) historians. They not only continued to flourish, however, in some early printed chronicles, such as the Nuremberg *Liber Chronicarum* (1493), in certain specialized categories of historiography, and in *Bilderbogen* or illustrated broadsides about recent or contemporary events, but made a significant comeback, in the nineteenth century, in popular histories for the new class of readers created by increasing economic prosperity and compulsory primary education, and in history textbooks for use in the schools of the nineteenth-century nation-states. Representational images also re-emerged, moreover, in a new form and with a new function, in the work of modern scholarly historians, often in conjunction with statistical graphs. A substantial section (section 8) was added to the original essay in order to take account of these later developments in the historiographical use of representational images.

I

Image and Story

For centuries, in all parts of the world, visual images have been used to evoke, adorn, or enliven stories—most often, at first, stories generally held to be in some sense "true," such as myths and histories important to particular communities. Single images in manuscript illuminations, for instance, have vividly brought to life particular key moments or actions in the textual narratives in which they are embedded [figs. I*, 1–9][1]. As the still image, by its nature, is incapable of directly representing movement, change, or the passage of time, however, visual representations of historical scenes have had to be content to allude to or suggest the stories that extend both before and after the particular moment they represent.

In a number of cases, such as Memling's remarkable *Passion of Christ* (1471; now in the Galleria Sabauda in Turin) and *The Seven Joys of the Virgin* (1480; Alte Pinakothek, Munich), artists have contrived to overcome the limitations of the still image by depicting or at least evoking successive moments or episodes on the same canvas as part of a single composition[2] [figs. II*, 10–13]. The once-common form of the triptych sometimes served the same purpose [figs. 14, 15]. More ambitious attempts to tell a story pictorially have involved the use of multiple images arranged in a series intended to be viewed successively. This was the method used in antiquity to repre-

---

[1] Roman numbers refer to illustrations in the printed text; numbers with an asterisk to illustrations in the color insert. Arabic numbers refer to illustrations in the online-only portfolio, http://www.amphilsoc.org/sites/default/files/Transactions_101_4.pdf

[2] On the so-called "Überschaubild," in which several different episodes are compressed into a "simultaneous narration," see the remarkable study of Philip Benedict, *Graphic History: The "Wars, Massacres and Troubles" of Tortorel and Perrissin* (Geneva: Droz, 2007), p. 77. A particularly interesting example is an image of Isaiah by the Nazarene artist Julius Schnorr von Carolsfeld (fig. 13), in which the lower part of the work presents the figure of Isaiah and the upper part the story of Christ from birth through crucifixion to resurrection, as foretold (in the figurative reading of the Old Testament) by the Old Testament prophet. Here historical succession is combined with typological repetition. (See the ingenious analysis of this work in Cordula Grewe, *Painting the Sacred in the Age of Romanticism* [Farnham, Surrrey: Ashgate, 2009], pp. 39–43; see also her discussion, pp. 232–33, of an illustration [fig. 12] by Schnorr in which events in the past that are the subject of speech in the scene represented are themselves represented in "balloons" within the image.) What is abundantly clear is the impossibility of deciphering Schnorr's complex and dense image without thorough knowledge of the texts and even of the theological interpretations of the texts.

sent episodes from Greek mythology,[3] and in South and Southeast Asia episodes from the Rāmāyana and Mahābhāratā epics and the life of the Buddha.[4] Episodes from the Old and New Testaments were represented in the same way on stained glass windows and in the sculptural programs on the walls and doors of medieval religious buildings,[5] on secular buildings,[6] as well as on scrolls such as the ten-meter-long Byzantine scroll depicting the events of the Book of Joshua (tenth century)[7] [figs. 16–18]. Since the invention of print, a vigorous tradition of serial images in so-called Bibles in pictures extends from the the *Biblia Pauperum* of the fifteenth and sixteenth centuries[8] and the productions of the Lyons printers and illustrators of the 1550s to a new high point in the mid-nineteenth century in the work of Julius Schnorr von Carolsfeld and Gustave Doré, and continues down to the present time[9] [figs. III, 19–24]. It has usually been assumed that images took

---

[3]As, for example, on the frieze of the Siphnian Treasury (6th Century B.C.), the Parthenon pediment, or the Telephos frieze from Pergamon (early 2nd Century B.C.), as well as on urns, sarcophagi, bowls, vases, etc. (4th and 5th century B.C.)

[4]See Marijke J. Klokke, *Narrative Sculpture and Literary Traditions in South and Southeast Asia*, Intro. by Jan Fontein (Leiden/Boston/Cologne: Brill, 2000). The use of visual material by historians as source or evidence raises different questions from those to be touched on here. On that topic, see Francis Haskell, *History and its Images* (New Haven: Yale University Press, 1993) and the short essay of Sarah Barber, "Fine Art: The Creative Image," in *History Beyond the Text: A Student's Guide to Approaching Alternative Sources* (London and New York: Routledge, 2009), pp. 15–31. In the same volume, Jeffrey Richards discusses film as a source for the historian, rather than as itself a medium of historiography ("Film and Television: The Moving Image," pp. 72–88).

[5]For instance, the doors of the abbey church of St. Michael in Hildesheim (1015) or the Ghiberti doors of the Battistero in Florence (15th Century), or the Christ story depicted in the stained glass windows of Chartres.

[6]As in the Joseph cycle painted (1815–17) by the Nazarene artists, Peter Cornelius, Friedrich Overbeck, Wilhelm Schadow, and Philipp Veit, in the so-called Casa Bartholdy (Casa Zuccari) for Salomon Bartholdy, the Prussian Consul-General in Rome.

[7]Codex Vaticanus Pal. Graec. 431.

[8]The *Biblia pauperum* ('Paupers' Bible') was a tradition of picture Bibles beginning in the later Middle Ages. Unlike illustrated Bibles, in which the image is subordinate to the text, the *Biblia pauperum* placed the image at the centre, with only a brief text or no text at all. Words spoken by the figures in the miniatures were sometimes written on scrolls coming out of their mouths. The origin of the term "Biblia pauperum" is uncertain, but it clearly did not mean Bibles for the poor. At first the *Biblia pauperum* took the form of colourful hand-painted illuminated manuscripts on vellum, which had to be very expensive. In the fifteenth century printed examples with woodcuts took over. These were cheaper and may have been affordable by parish priests for use as a teaching aid.

[9]On the Lyons printers, see Benedict, *Graphic History*, p. 82. Schnorr von Carolsfeld's *Die Bibel in Bildern*, with 240 images, first published in Leipzig in 1860, went through many subsequent editions in German and in translation (see Grewe, *Painting the Sacred*, pp. 246–49). Gustave Doré's illustrated Bible, with over 200 images, was first published in 1866 and has continued to be republished, in many languages, ever since. The genre of the Bible in Pictures shows no sign of fading. Recent versions include Josephine Pollard, *The Bible and Its Story*, with 280 illustrations in the style of Schnorr (New York/London/Glasgow/Manchester: George Routledge, 1890); *The Bible in Pictures,* (New York: Francis R. Niglutsch, 1908–10) by two academic historians, Charles F. Horne and Julius A. Bewer, in ten volumes, with countless illustrations, each one the focus of a particular episode and its relevant text in the Old and New Testaments, by artists ranging from the painters of the Renaissance down to Loutherbourg, Blake, the Nazarene artists Joseph Führich and Jullius Schnorr von Carolsfeld,

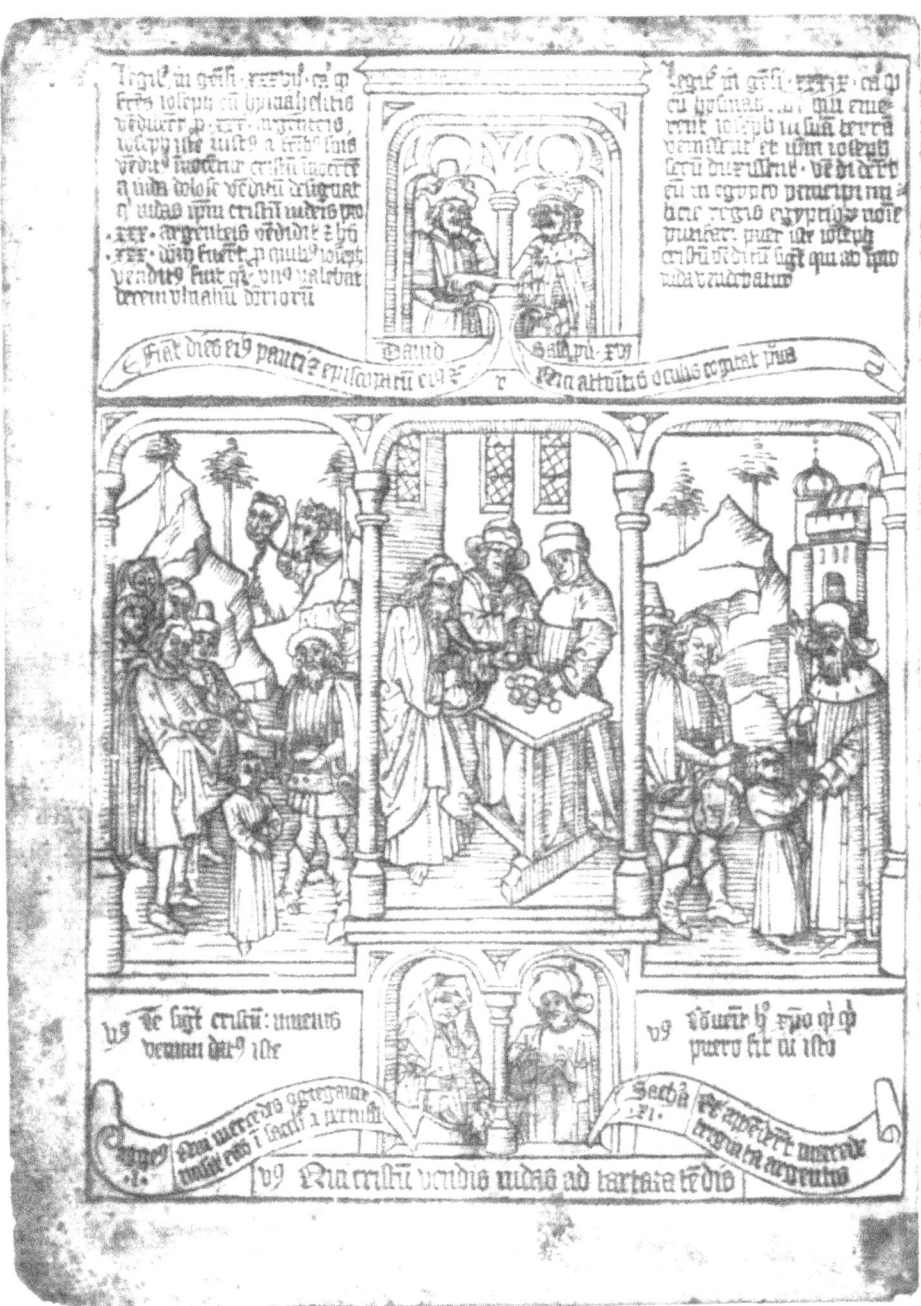

FIGURE III *Biblia Pauperum* (Netherlands , circa 1465). Block book, sheet 17. "Judas is paid" in center, flanked by "Joseph is sold to the Ishmaelites" and "Joseph is sold to Potiphar." By kind permission of the British Museum, London. © British Museum.

the place of texts, especially for children and the illiterate. In the words of Guillaume Durand, the thirteenth-century Bishop of Mende, "Pictures are the letters and scriptures of the laity."[10]

Serial images were also used for secular historical narratives, as on Trajan's column in Rome (early second century), with its presentation of the history of the two Dacian wars in 155 successive scenes spiraling (less and less visibly!) up the column toward the triumphal figure of Trajan at the top;[11] the twelfth-century Bayeux Tapestry, whose 32 scenes embroidered on a 70-meter roll of cloth depict successive moments in William of Normandy's invasion of England; the thirteenth-century Charlemagne window at Chartres with its scenes from the story of Roland; or the remarkable series of thirty-nine prints by Jacques Tortorel and Jean Perrissin that depict "Les Guerres, Massacres & Troubles advenus en France en ces dernieres annees" (i.e. the Wars of Religion in France and the events leading up to them), published in Geneva in 1569–1570 and supposedly based on "le tesmoignage de ceux qui y ont este en personne, & et qui les ont veus" ["the testimony of those who were there in person and have seen the events depicted"][12] [figs. IV*, V, 25–32]. Numerous tapestry and print series were created in the sixteenth and seventeenth centuries to represent and celebrate the exploits of early modern monarchs [fig. 33].[13] In 1573 a set of 108 numbered images based on Livy's Roman History, each with a title and brief accompanying verse text, was published in Frankfurt as *Icones Livianae* or *Neuwe livische Figuren* by Zurich woodcutter Jost Amman. In

---

Gustave Doré, and James Tissot; Lillie A. Faris's multi-volume *Bible Story Readers*, illustrated by O.A. Stemler and Bess B. Cleveland (Standard Publishing Co., 1925–29); and *The Bible in Pictures*, with illustrations by Max Bihn and James Bealings (Chicago and Toronto: John A. Hertel Co., 1912), in which the text has to be completed by words suggested by the images inserted into the text in comic book or puzzle style. Kenneth Taylor's *The Bible in Pictures for Little Eyes* (Moody Press, 1912), directed as the title suggsts at the very young, has gone through countless editions since it first appeared and is still being republished. As recently as 1994, *Jesus of Nazareth: A Life of Christ through Pictures, Illustrated with Paintings from the National Gallery of Art, Washington, D.C.*, was put out by the New York publishing firm of Simon and Schuster.

[10]"Pictura et ornamenta in ecclesia sunt laicorum lectiones et scripturae." One of three epigraphs in Herbert Kessler and Marianne Shreve Simpson, eds., *Pictorial Narrative in Antiquity and the Middle Ages* (Washington: National Gallery of Art, 1985; Studies in the History of Art, vol. 16).

[11]"A new feeling for the importance of specific historical events" in Hellenistic and post-Hellenistic art is attributed by the Harvard classical scholar George M.A. Hanfmann to "the deeds of Alexander and his successors. Such myth-rivalling careers called for detailed reporting which could best be achieved by unfolding their stories in detailed 'cyclic' sequences. A new feeling for concreteness, variety, and largeness of the *oikoumene* called for settings in which symbolic generality would yield to a convincing portrayal of large, recognizable locations." ("Narration in Greek Art," *American Journal of Archaeology*, 61 [1957]: 71–78, on p. 77) The story of the Dacian wars as depicted on Trajan's column reappeared in pictorial form as the subject of a series of 140 prints published in Rome in the 1560s and 1570s. (See Benedict, *Graphic History*, p. 83).

[12]The central subject of Philip Benedict's, *Graphic History* (see note 2 above).

[13]On the proliferation in the fourteenth and fifteenth centuries of "cycles dedicated to relatively recent events of profane history [. . .] in many forms, including tapestries, frescoes, tomb relief sculptures, *cassone*, and manuscript illuminations," see Benedict, *Graphic History*, p. 76,

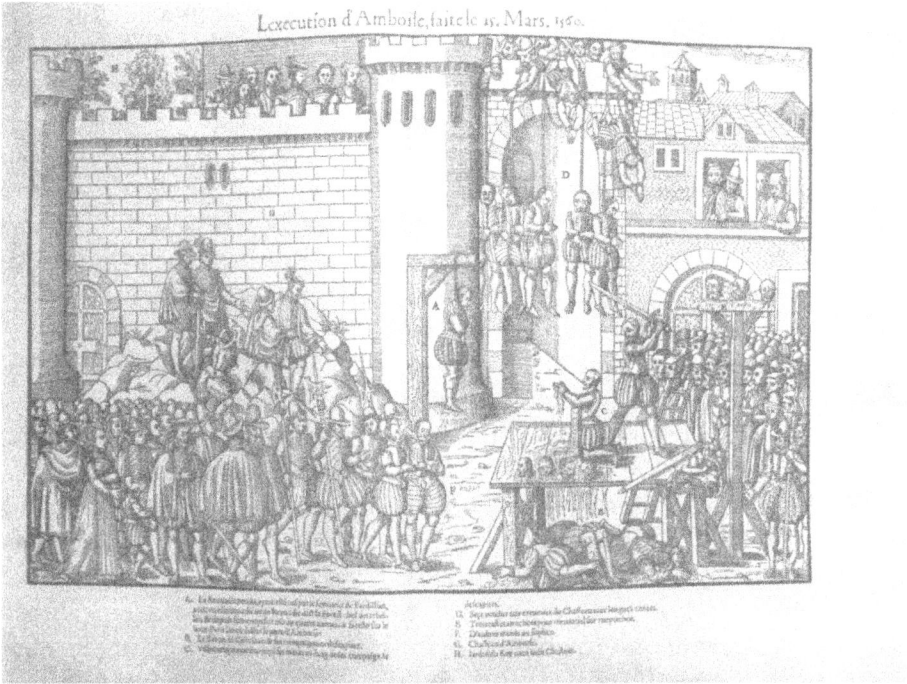

FIGURE V "L'exécution d'Amboise," from Jacques Tortorel and Jean Perrissin, *Quarante Tableaux ou Histoires diverses qui sont memorables touchant les Guerres, Massacres et Troubles advenus en France en ces dernieres annees. Le tout recueilly selon le tesmoignage de ceux qui y ont este en personne et qui les ont veus* (Geneva, 1570). In Alfred Franklin, ed., *Les Grandes Scènes Historiques du XVIème siècle*, Reproduction facsimilé du receuil de J. Tortorel et J. Perrissin (Paris: Librairie Fischbacher, 1886), Plate X. Princeton University Library.

some unusual works designed to teach history, images represent the point of departure rather than an illustration or ornamentation of a text. In a pocket-sized German work that appears to date from the early nineteenth century, over 100 engravings depicting selected events from biblical times to the Napoleonic era (fig. 34) give rise to one or two pages of narrative; taken together, these images and their accompanying texts constitute links in the chain of universal history.[14] In a more recent and far weightier 22-volume set, *The Great Events by Famous Historians*, images again precede the verbal narratives—most of the latter taken from eminent nineteenth- and early-twentieth century historians. Here too, though the narratives are far longer than in the little German book, the images appear primary (figs. 35–37). Instead of the image's ornamenting the narrative, the narrative appears to be generated by the image.[15]

---

[14]This work belonged to the grandmother of my friend and colleague, the historian Peter Paret. Unfortunately, the title page has been lost.

[15]Full title: *The Great Events by Famous Historians; A Comprehensive and Readable Account of the World's History, Emphasizing the More Important Events, and Presenting These as Complete Narratives in the Master-words of the Most Eminent Historians*. Compiled by a staff of editors headed by Charles F. Horne and John Rudd ([New York]: The National Alumni,1926). Horne was also the editor of a *Bible in Pictures*; see note 9 above.

Nevertheless, the common view has been that most storytelling images, including serial images, are dependent for their interpretation on the viewer's prior knowledge of the relevant verbal narrative or on a narrative text accompanying and explaining the image.[16] The images used to tell of some striking or shocking recent or contemporary event in the popular prints and broadsides or *Bilderbogen* of the fifteenth through the nineteenth centuries and even into the twentieth—which can be seen as forerunners not only of the comic strip but of twentieth-century picture magazines, such as *Picture Post* in the United Kingdom and *Life* in the United States—are invariably accompanied by a textual narrative, even if the text is unquestionably subordinate to the image. [figs. VI, VII*, VIII*, IX*, X, 38–48]. Unlike their modern photojournalism counterparts, moreover, these images were almost always based on a prior narrative text.[17] In classical antiquity, it has been suggested, some visual representations (for example, those on the so-called Megarian bowls) served as a kind of aide-mémoire for the epic or dramatic narratives of which the viewer was expected to have some knowledge.[18] A somewhat similar function appears to have been attributed to prints in the early modern period on the grounds that, as Philip Benedict explains, "even when historical events were communicated in words, authors urged their readers to form mental images of them, the better to remember and be inspired by them."[19] In sum, decoding the visual image in narrative art as one scholar put it, "presupposes familiarity with the texts"[20]—or at least with a verbal narrative. An authority on Babylonian art concurs: "Of course, it is essential that the beholder be familiar with the story."[21] A similar view is also expressed by a recent writer on the use of biblical imagery in the early modern period. Questioning Luther's claim that images accompanying his cate-

---

[16]Some scholars have begun investigating the structures, techniques, and opportunities peculiar to visual (as distinct from verbal) narratives; see especially Richard Brilliant, *Visual Narratives: Storytelling in Etruscan and Roman Art* (Ithaca and London: Cornell University Press, 1984).

[17]Benedict, *Graphic History*, p. 103.

[18]Brilliant, *Visual Narratives*, p. 42. Similarly, an *image d'Epinal* devoted to the story of Puss in Boots functions in many ways as a reminder of the story rather than an actual telling of it.

[19]Benedict, *Graphic History*, pp. 98–100.

[20]Marijke J. Klokke, "The Krsna reliefs at Panataran. A Visual Version of the Old Javanese Krsnāyana," in Klokke, *Narrative Sculpture*, p.19. In a recent article ("Time, the Infinite Storyteller") in the *New York Times* (1.1.2011) one of the paper's art critics, Roberta Smith, notes that "Sometimes a narrative is so deeply embedded in cultural consciousness that [the depiction of] a single moment from it, or maybe two—as in a before and after—can stand for the epic whole." (p. C-28) Though Benedict (see note 2 above) believes Tortorel and Perrissin may have produced "the first extended print series offering a pictorial account of recent events where the images do not simply illustrate a written history but carry the burden of telling the story themselves" (p. 4), each image nonetheless carried a title along with the date of the event portrayed, as well as a key to the objects or persons represented. In addition, the events were recent enough for oral narratives of them to be in circulation and Benedict himself lists several pre-existing printed accounts of each event.

[21]Anne Perkins, "Narrative in Babylonian Art," *American Journal of Archaeology*, 1957, 61:54–62, on p. 55, note 6. This point was made by James Harris in his "Treatise the Second" in *Three Treatises, The First Concerning Art, The Second Concerning Music, Painting, and Poetry, the Third Concerning Happiness* (1744): "A Picture being [. . .] but a *Point* or *Instant*, in

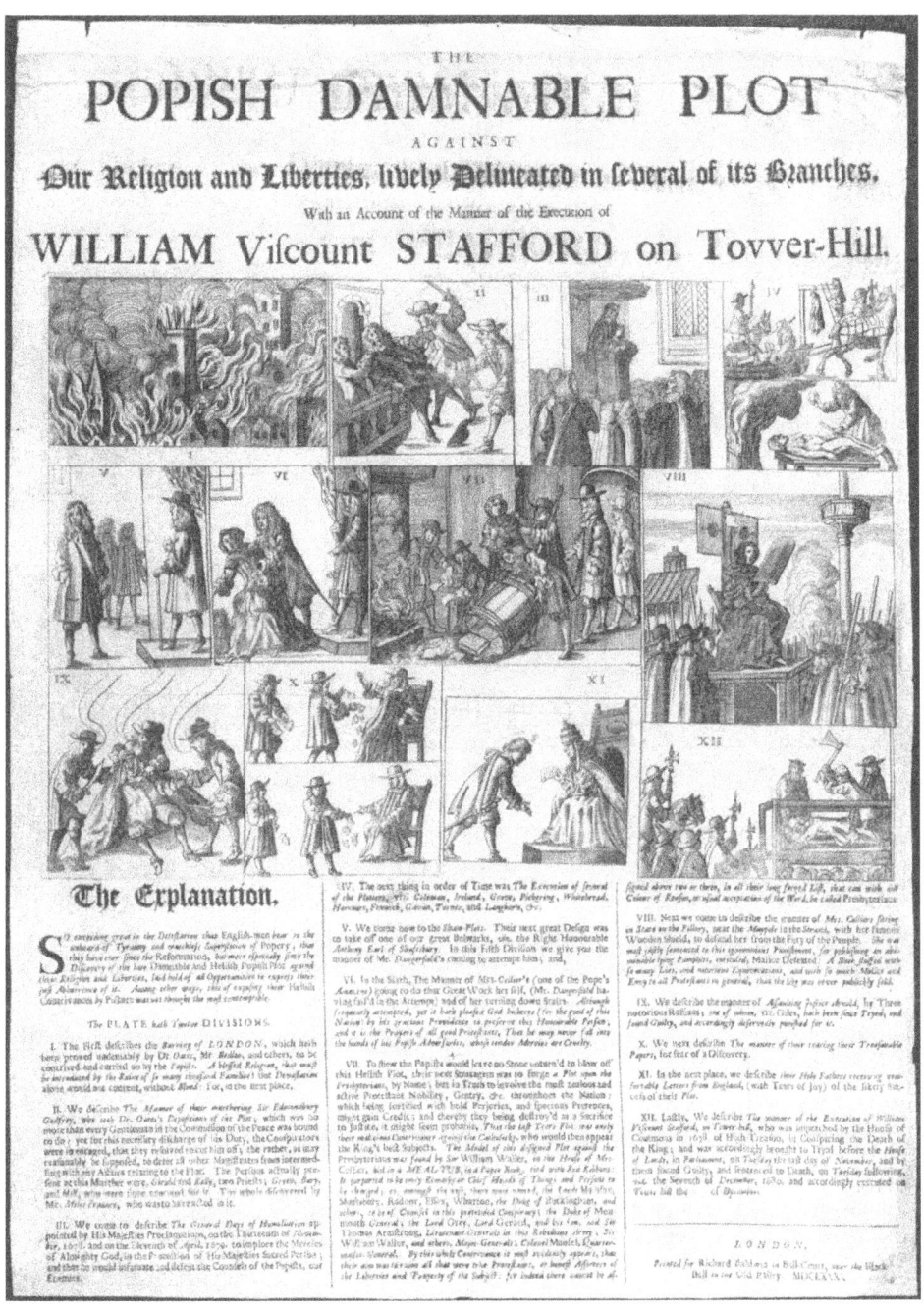

FIGURE VI "The Popish Damnable Plot." Broadside printed for Richard Baldwin, London, 1680. By kind permission of the British Library. © British Library Board. Shelf no. C..20.f.xiii,142.

a Story *well known* the Spectator's Memory will supply the *previous* and the *subsequent*. But this cannot be done, *where such Knowledge is wanting*. And therefore it may be justly questioned, whether the most celebrated Subjects, borrowed by Painting from History, would have been any of them intelligible *thro' the Medium of Painting only*, supposing History to have been silent, and to have given *no additional Information*." (4th ed. [London: C. Noursse, 1783], ch. II, note [h], pp. 64–65; see note 25 below.)

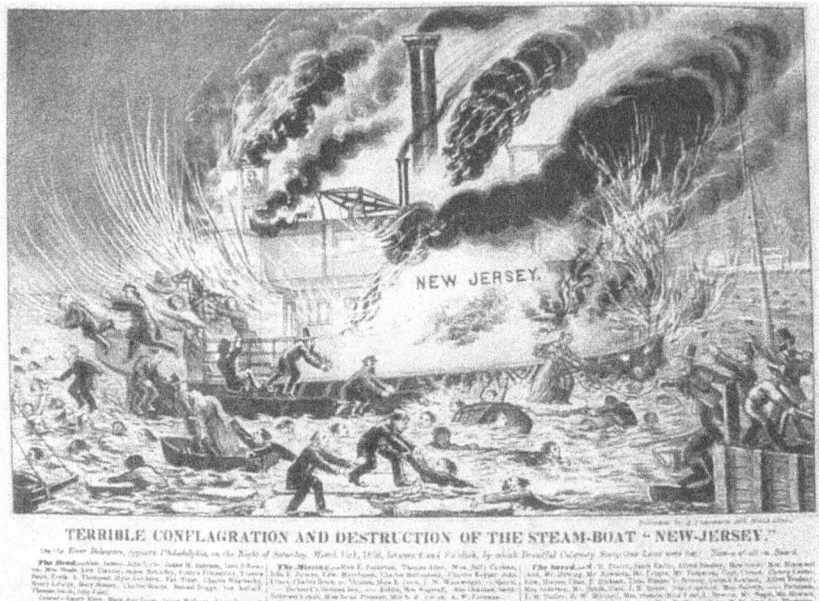

Caption area within image:

TERRIBLE CONFLAGRATION AND DESTRUCTION OF THE STEAM-BOAT "NEW-JERSEY."

FIGURE X "Terrible Conflagration and Destruction of the Steam-Boat 'New Jersey'." Popular lithographic print (1856). Philadelphia: A. Pharazin, 1856. Courtesy of the Philadelphia Print Shop, Ltd., Philadelphia, PA.

chism would be useful to "Kinder und einfeltigen," Gerhard Ringshausen argues that "children and simple people were precisely those least capable of understanding illustrations of the catechism, in as much as they might well not have possessed the requisite knowledge of the Bible. Conditions for understanding images existed only in those sectors of the population that were literate and could expand their religious culture through the reading of sermons and books of devotion, which themselves made use of images."[22]

This widely-held view about the dependency of the image on the viewer's knowledge of a preexisting or accompanying verbal narrative may need to be nuanced.

Hogarth's eight-picture series of "A Rake's Progess" (now in Sir John Soane's Museum in London) and six-picture series of "The Harlot's Progress" (destroyed in a fire but known to us from engravings) purport to tell a sequential story without reference to any particular preexisting narrative, though not without short titles evoking a generic narrative. Art historian Wolfgang Kemp acknowledges that intervals between the successive still images inevitably persist in both series and that these intervals invalidate

---

[22]Gerhard Ringshausen, *Von der Buchillustration zum Unterrichtsmedium* (Weinheim and Basel: Beltz, 1976), p. 39. (All translations from German and French are by L.G. unless otherwise stated.) Cf. René Dewil, *The Art of Painting* (www.theartofpainting.be): "The paintings of the Gothic Middle Ages in Flanders were full of narrative scenes and symbols. [. . .] The clergy only had the theological knowledge to explain the pictures. [. . .] The clergy thus showed that only they had the keys to an understanding of the scriptures; they could show that they always knew something more of the Gospels than the common folk and they benefited from the reputation. They were supposed to be more close to the saints and the Virgin Mary."

Hogarth's comparison of his images to the pages of a book. At the same time, however, Kemp demonstrates that the intervals are transformed in Hogarth' series from a narrative handicap into a productive device—not unlike the blanks sometimes deliberately left by writers of narrative—for stimulating the viewer's imagination and enhancing the dramatic effect of the complete narrative.[23] Modern "novels in pictures," such as Frans Masereel's *De Stad* (1925) and *Die Passion eines Menschen* (1927), Otto Nückel's *Schicksal* (1930) or Lynd Ward's *God's Man* (1930) and his extremely complex *Vertigo* (1937) continue the Hogarthian tradition in a new form.

Even free-standing, non-serial narrative paintings, moreover, may refer to no established pre-existing narrative but instead invite the viewer to *invent* a narrative relevant to the moment represented in the image and to the (usually laconic) title provided for it, as Diderot's commentary on Greuze's *Jeune fille qui pleure son oiseau mort* in his review of the Salon of 1765 demonstrates.[24] Ford Madox Brown's "The Last of England" (1853), painted at the height of nineteenth-century emigration from England (several of the artists' friends had emigrated and he himself thought he might have to), may well have encouraged each individual viewer to read his or her own emigration story out of it [fig. 49]. Géricault's "Le Radeau de la Méduse" (1817–18) alluded to an event that had indeed been widely reported—the shipwreck of the *Medusa* with 400 people on board off the coast of Senegal on July 2, 1816—but about which no canonical narrative existed. The account of the event published in 1817 by two of the survivors, the surgeon Savigny and the engineer Corréard, was hardly in everybody's hands. Géricault's image thus stimulated the viewer to create his or her own narrative.

What was widely believed, especially since the influential theoretical writings of G.E. Lessing and his English predecessor James Harris in the eighteenth century, to be the chief handicap of the visual image as a narrative medium—namely the discreteness that limits it to the representation of the *Nebeneinander* (elements co-present at a single moment in time) and renders it incapable of representing the *Nacheinander* (succession and change)[25]—

---

[23]Wolfgang Kemp, "Ellipsen, Analepsen, Gleichzeitigkeiten: Schwierige Aufgaben für die Bilderzählung," in Wolfgang Kemp, ed., *Der Text des Bildes. Möglichkeiten und Mittel eigentümlicher Bilderzählung* (Munich: Text + Kritik, 1989), pp. 62–68.

[24]*Salons*, ed. Jean Seznec and Jean Adhémar (Oxford: Clarendon Press, 1960), vol. 2, pp. 145-48.

[25]Lessing's celebrated argument, summarized in *Laokoon* (1766), Section XVI, was anticipated by a few years in a now neglected work by the ingenious English polymath, James Harris. In his "Treatise the Second" in *Three Treatises, The First Concerning Art, The Second Concerning Music, Painting, and Poetry, The Third Concerning Happiness* of 1744 (see note 20 above), Harris assumes that all the arts "agree, by being *all* MIMETIC, or IMITATIVE. They *differ*, as they imitate by *different Media*: PAINTING by *Figure* and *Colour*; MUSIC, by *Sound* and *Motion*; PAINTING and MUSIC, by *Media which are Natural*; POETRY, for the greatest Part, by a *Medium which is Artificial*." (4th ed., Ch. I, p. 58) He then goes on to distinguish the particular strengths of each of the arts and the "subjects" best suited to it. "The *Subjects of Poetry*," he argues, "to which the Genius of *Painting* is *not adapted*, are—all Actions whose *Whole* is of so *lengthened* a Duration, that *no Point of Time*, in any part of that Whole, can be given *fit for painting*; neither in its *Beginning*, which will teach what is *Subsequent*; nor in its *End*,

was finally removed with the arrival of the "motion" picture.[26] The intervals between the individual frames of a film having become imperceptible, sudden transitions and narrative blanks became as much an artistic device for the narrator in cinematic images (rather than an essential impediment of the medium) as they have always been for the narrator in words. The silent film already succeeded in vividly representing—and not just suggesting—continuous action, movement, change, and the passage of time, and was only minimally dependent on text (in the form of occasional titles) for its interpretation by the viewer. Enjoying, in addition, the advantages of sound, modern movies are capable of successfully transposing the narrative content of any verbal work into cinematic terms, as the custom of making film versions of classic and popular novels testifies. It is even possible to create something like a visual equivalent—by means of lighting, camera angle, cross-cutting, cutaway shots, and similar techniques—of one of the essential elements of all verbal narrative, the narrator's explicit or implicit commentary on the action (*discours*, as distinct from *récit*, in the useful terminology of Emile Benveniste). Historical movies, such as Clint Eastwood's *Letters from Iwo Jima* (2006) or Michael Haneke's *Das weisse Band* (2009), are no different in this respect from historical novels. In historical documentaries, such as Roberto Rossellini's *La Prise de Pouvoir par Louis XIV* (made for Italian TV) or Ken Burns' *The Civil War* (made for PBS in the United States), in which the element of *discours* is as dominant as in historiographical writing, *discours* is communicated both verbally and visually. At the same time, however, the limited success of early picture series in representing change over time and the complete success of the technologically advanced motion picture or film have had to be purchased at the cost of sacrificing an essential feature of the single still image—that it conveys a highly concentrated message immediately, without having to unfold in time.

---

which will teach what is *Previous*; nor in its *Middle*, which will declare both the *Previous* and the *Subsequent*." (Ch. V, pp. 83–84) In other words, as painting cannot represent "the Whole," the picture itself cannot narrate. The argument of Lessing and Harris can still be discerned in a recent study of the increasingly popular historical museum. Historical museums, according to Michael Jeissmann, "lack historiographical competency inasmuch as they can display historical objects and even stage them, but cannot truly narrate history [. . .] 'History,' however, always implies 'narration'; it always means making visible what cannot be shown: contexts, reflections, relations. The museum, on the other hand, is primarily concerned with showing. Narration is secondary, supplementary, incidental, unoriginal in every respect, in sharp contrast to the objects." ("Über angeschaute und erzählte Geschichte. Die pränarrative Situation des Museums," in Martin Padberg, Martin Schmidt, eds., *Die Magie der Geschichte: Geschichtskultur und Museum* [Bielefeld: transcript-Verlag, 2010], pp. 53-59, on p. 55)

[26]It might be objected that dramatic representations, spoken or mimed (as in the celebrated scene in *Hamlet*), already constituted an effective visual narrative of events. Unlike the moving picture, however, the dramatic performance is a re-enactment rather than a depiction.

II

Non-representational Visualizations of History: Maps, Genealogical Trees, Chronological Tables

Telling, or at least evoking, a story in images that represent events and actions, has not, however, been the only way in which the visual has contributed to historiography.[27] Maps, for instance, have had an important place in historical writing since earliest times because of their ability to provide certain kinds of information about the setting of actions in the past far more quickly and precisely than either a verbal description or *a fortiori* a representational image of what the eye might actually have beheld at any given place and moment. It is possible that the Second Century B.C. Jewish Book of Jubilees was accompanied by a map and that there was a cartographic tradition in Hebrew biblical commentary. Mappings of the Holy Land certainly survive in manuscripts dating from the thirteenth to the fifteenth century.[28] Maps were especially characteristic of Reformation bibles, and at the time of the Renaissance, as emphasis fell more and more on the

---

[27]The invaluable study of Anthony Grafton and Daniel Rosenberg, *Cartographies of Time* (Princeton Architectural Press, 2010) appeared just after I had completed this article. I was thus unfortunately unable to take advantage of it.

[28]Jeremy Black, *Maps and History: Constructing Images of the Past* (New Haven and London: Yale University Press, 1997), pp. 4–10; Francis Schmidt, "Naissance d'une géographie juive," in *Moïse géographe*, ed. Alain Desreumaux and Francis Schmidt (Paris: Vrin, 1988), pp. 13–30, on pp. 19, 22. However, A. and G. Waijntraub, *Hebrew Maps of the Holy Land* (Vienna: Brüder Hollinek, 1992) point out that the illustrators of Rashi's eleventh century commentary of the Pentateuch in some extant thirteenth century manuscripts were clearly unfamiliar with cartographic practice and illustrated the text rather with schematic diagrams (*Yitzur* or *Tsura*) of the Holy Land.

literal as opposed to the allegorical interpretation of both Holy Scripture and the Greek and Roman Classics, maps came increasingly to figure in writings on Judeo-Christian history and on classical antiquity. By the seventeenth century, maps were a feature of some texts dealing with modern history.[29] In addition to illustrating and enriching historical texts, historical maps also functioned as a visual means of communicating historical information independently of texts. The first historical atlas, as such, is usually said to be the *Parergon* of Abraham Ortelius (1527–98), published as a supplement to his *Theatrum Orbis Terrarum* of 1570 (generally regarded as "the first modern atlas") and then in a final, full version as a separate book (Antwerp, 1624).[30] In one of Ortelius's maps the Biblical story of Abraham's journey to the Promised Land is evoked by a combination of geographical representation and serial pictorial images [fig. 50]. As Jeremy Black has shown, maps have thus played an independent role in shaping people's conceptions of the past.[31] Still, like visual representations of events, maps normally present a stationary view of a situation at any one given time, and are not particularly suited to the representation of change and the passage of time. At best, like Memling's *Passion of Christ*, they may—by means of color, shading, and numerical dating—provide elements from which the viewer can construct or reconstruct a story or development that is not actually represented [fig. 51]. Generally speaking, maps communicate momentary or successive structures rather than the dynamic of change [fig. 52].

Genealogical trees, beginning with the popular Jesse trees on stained glass windows and in medieval manuscripts, might appear to come somewhat closer to representing time spatially than either images of actions or maps. While displaying connections across time, however, they are not primarily concerned with time as such. Indeed, their function might be rather to provide a visual demonstration of relations that are "in time," but unaffected by it. The intervals between individual entries are unimportant in themselves because time itself is unimportant—just as it is in figural or allegorical histories, where one actor or action "prefigures" a later one. What counts is not so much time or change as the persistence of an essence through time. Hence, no effort is usually made to represent the length of time that has elapsed from one generation to the next or the differences that distinguish each generation from the others [figs. 53, 54].

In some branches of historical writing the visual layout of the text on the page played a significant role. Since their primary object is to establish the temporal order of succession itself rather than to describe the content of the items arranged in order, chronological tables strove to represent

---

[29]As in John Speed's "Briefe Description of the Civil Wares and Battails fought in England, Wales, and Ireland" (in his *A Prospect of the Most Famous Parts of the World* [London, 1627]), which was illustrated by a double-page black and white map of "The Invasions of England and Ireland with all their civil wars since the Conquest."

[30]Black, *Maps and History*, pp. 4–10.

[31]Black's *Maps and History* provides an excellent account of the way maps have shaped understanding of the past from ancient times to the present.

time in space by compressing long periods of time into a single page, which could be viewed at one glance, and on which the passage of time would be represented by the vertical succession of dates (usually in the left margin). By the mid-eighteenth century some chronologies had become quite rich and complex, especially after color was added, toward the end of the century and in the early nineteenth century, to underline continuities and connections [figs. 55–56]. Moreover, at a time when historians were calling for a larger, more inclusive vision of the past than that offered by either the traditional Christian account of universal history or the more recent dynastic and national histories—a history that would embrace not only the actions of political and military leaders, but the achievements of inventors, artists, and scientists, not only politics but culture, not only the world of Christendom but the entire inhabited world—chronologies were well placed, precisely because of their relation to the visual, to make the simultaneity and, to a limited degree, the potential interconnectedness of diverse historical series immediately and vividly perceptible. Narrative history, in contrast, had great difficulty at first, because of its own particular constraints, in treating these simultaneous series otherwise than successively. If, as Harris and Lessing alleged, the visual image is tied to contiguity and simultaneity (the *Nebeneinander*) and cannot easily represent process or change (the *Nacheinander*), the narrative text is tied to the latter and cannot easily render the former; hence the frequently noted limitations of Voltaire's *Essai sur les moeurs* or Hume's *History*. Even as they aspired to integrate many more aspects of the past into their work than traditional histories, with their virtually exclusive emphasis on the actions of the great and powerful, on war and politics, Hume and Voltaire relegated the new aspects of history—commerce, culture, the arts—which were, in any case, less amenable to traditional narrative treatment, to special, separate chapters. In contrast, the horizontal bar on late eighteenth- and early nineteenth-century chronological tables ranged from Europe to the Near and Far East, and from politics to philosophy, science, and the arts, thus allowing for simultaneous representation of all.[32] In their range and diversity these works are comparable with fairly recent chronologies such as those of S.H. Steinberg (*Historical Tables* [London: Macmillan, 1939]), Jean Delorme (*Chronologie des civilisations* [Paris: P.U.F., 1949]), or Arno Peters (*Synchronoptische Weltgeschichte* [Munich and Hamburg: Universum, 1952) [figs. 57–59]. Peters himself emphasized that his intent was not unlike that of the Enlightenment historians at an earlier stage in the history of historiography. They wanted to extend the scope of history beyond the actions of the great and powerful to the silent activities of the anonymous builders of "civilization"; he wanted to extend the scope of

---

[32]As early as 1685 a popular and widely used chronology published by the learned Cambridge scholar Francis Tallents (*A view of Universal History from the Creation to the Destruction of Jerusalem by Adrian in the Year of the World 4084 and of Christ 135*) included in the horizontal bar, along with geographical and political divisions (Greece, Italy, Britain), categories such as "Philosophers," "Learned Men," and "Writers."

history beyond Europe and the known historical world to those parts of it often considered "history-less."

But chronological tables had their own drawbacks. In some cases (especially tables representing ancient history and those historical fields about which there was a paucity of information) the dates in the vertical timeline in the left margin were extremely irregular, so that the space between the dates in no way corresponded to the length of time between them. Even when a regular series of dates was used—virtually successive years, as in the later parts of the chronology of Nicolas Lenglet du Fresnoy (*Tables chronologiques de l'histoire universelle* [Paris: Pierre Gandouin, 1729; revised eds. 1744, 1763, 1778, Engl. trans. 1762]), the post-medieval parts of P. N. Chantreau's ambitious *Science de l'Histoire . . . développée par tableaux synoptiques* (Paris: Goujon fils, An XI [1803]) or Ernst Fischer's *Römische Zeittafeln* (Altona: J.F. Hammerich, 1846)—the space attributed to each year varied according to the amount of information provided; once again, there was no direct correspondence between time and its spatial or visual representation [figs. 60–65].

In a few cases, however, such a direct correspondence between space and time was maintained. John Blair's extremely popular *The Chronology and History of the World: from the Creation to the Year of Christ 1753* (London, 1754; numerous later editions, and a French translation by P.N. Chantreau, 1795), was organized by successive years, with each year occupying the same amount of space [fig. 66]. Divided into centuries, the chronological table appended to Adam Ferguson's article "History" in the second edition of the *Encyclopedia Britannica* (Edinburgh, 1780) likewise devoted exactly the same space to each century [fig. XI*, 67, 68], while John Luffman's table in his *Elements of History and Chronology* (London, 1805, 2nd ed. 1814) devoted the same space to each of the twenty-five year periods into which his chronology was divided. Major James Bell's updated version (London: Baldwin, Craddock and Joy, 1820) of the fifth edition of G. G. Bredow's *Weltgeschichte in Tabellen* (first ed., 1801) inscribed irregular dates in the margin, but maintained a strict equivalency of time and space[33] [fig. 69]. Laid on their sides, these tables would be quite similar to Jacques Barbeu-Dubourg's pioneering *Carte chronographique* (1753) or Joseph Priestley's celebrated *Chart of Biography* (1765). (Priestley seems in fact to have borrowed from Blair the categories of "Men of Learning or genius" and "Statesmen, warriors, etc.", which complemented in Blair's *Chronology and History of the World* the columns reserved for the names of the rulers of the various parts of the world and "Remarkable events.") The consequence of the layout adopted by Blair, Ferguson, and Luffman was, however, that either only the barest historical information was provided, even when much was avail-

---

[33]*Compendious view of universal history and literature, in a series of twenty tables [. . .] grounded on the fifth edition of the German of G.G. Bredow [. . .] to which is appended a table of painters, arranged in schools and ages, principally from the private French notes of Sir Matthew van Brée [. . .] the whole translated, with various alterations, and considerable additions [. . .] by Major James Bell, 4th ed. (London: T.C. Hansard, 1833).

able,[34] or the period covered by the chronology had to be itself strictly curtailed. Above all, chronologies did not represent change or development any more effectively than still images arranged in series. The years or centuries into which they were divided remained independent of each other. The items recorded were likewise disparate and each had to be read separately. Chronologies did not depict a development. What they provided was simply a cross-sectional view of rulers, leading men and women, and chief events at successive points in time. No attempt was made to represent a development over time that was significant in itself.

Joseph Priestley was keenly aware of the disadvantage of irregular temporal units. Comparing the 1685 chronological chart of Francis Tallents (*A View of Universal History from the Creation, to the Destruction of Jerusalem by Adrian, in the Year of the World 4084, and of Christ 135*), about which he had otherwise good things to say, with the earlier (1651) *Historical and Chronological Theatre* of Christoph Hellwig (Helvicus), Priestley noted that since Tallents used the same amount of space for the 70 years from 325 to 395 as for the 390 years between 1146 and 1536, the graphic element itself did not convey in his chart anything more temporally precise than chronological order. Helvicus, in contrast, disposed "events in such a manner, as that the distance at which they are placed, without attending to the date in the margin, shall give a just idea of the real interval of time between them." "This is done," he explained, "by having a single line, or any set space, appropriated to any set period of time, or number of years."[35]

The *Carte chronographique* (1753) of Jacques Barbeu-Dubourg—doctor, botanist, friend, and translator of Benjamin Franklin—was one of the earliest and most imaginative works in which time is accurately represented by space.[36] It featured a horizontal timeline engraved along the top of a continuous 54-foot-long paper scroll, with the years from "the creation of the

---

[34]Ferguson presented this as his considered choice: "The dates are taken chiefly from that comprehensive and useful work, Blair's Chronological Tables. Use has likewise been made of the Chart of Universal History, formed on a design like this, but differently executed. Compared to that chart, the present may be thought incomplete. Nor would it have been difficult for the gentleman who sketched it to have filled it up with remarkable events, successions of kings, and lives of men; but he preferred clearness and simplicity, leaving to every person the filling up of his own plan with such articles as are most in the way of his curiosity and study. He has contented himself with a few specimens of this sort, in the succession of the Roman emperors, of the kings of England and France; and in the lives of one or two remarkable men, as in those of Tacitus the Historian, and Atilla. One person may choose to fill his plan with the names of statesmen and warriors, another with scholars and men of letters. To attempt inserting all that deserve being recorded, would crowd and embarrass the whole."

[35]See Daniel Rosenberg, "Joseph Priestley and the Graphic Invention of Modern Time," *Studies in Eighteenth Century Culture*, 36 (2007): 55-103, citing on p. 74 Joseph Priestley, *Lectures on History and General Policy to Which is Prefixed An Essay on a Course on Liberal Education for a Civil and Active Life* (London: J. Johnson, 1788). Helvicus, in turn, was faulted, Rosenberg notes, for being more concerned with juxtaposing and comparing different chronological systems than with the flow of history itself.

[36]For a full account, see Stephen Ferguson, "The 1753 *Carte chronographique* of Jacques Barbeu-Dubourg," *Princeton University Library Chronicle*, 52 (1990–91): 190–230.

world" to Dubourg's own time[37] marked off in small, equal, one-year incre-
ments. (The spatial length of one year was about 2.5 mm.) Decades were
marked by perpendicular lines. The space below the horizontal timeline was
divided into segments reserved for different categories of information: rulers
by country, "événements" of various kinds, and "personnages." Into that
space Dubourg inscribed not only the relevant rulers and reigns, not only
invasions, wars, battles, treaties, rebellions, and revolutions, but geographic
discoveries, scientific inventions, notable works of engineering, the founding of academies, and not only kings, princes, and great military figures, but
writers and artists, philosophers, and scientists. The "personnages"
(inscribed at the point of birth) were identified not only by name but by a
complex system of symbols indicating both the activity for which they were
known (e.g. "admiral," "artist," "assassin," "chemist" "conqueror," "geographer," "judge," "monk," "minister," "poisoner," "prophet," "saint," "savant,"
"sailor") and a moral characterization (e.g. "cruel," "impious," "rich and
greedy," "wicked and unjust"). Though it was also available for sale in separate sheets, Dubourg's *Carte chronographique* was envisaged by its creator
as a scroll housed in a specially designed "machine"—described in great
detail by Diderot in his article "Chronologique (Machine)" in the third volume of the *Encylopédie*—which allowed it to be wound and unwound at the
viewer's convenience [fig. 70]. Wherever the user of the machine stopped,
the visible "screen" area between the two cylinders of the machine exposed
a period of about 140 years. Thanks to Dubourg's scroll and machine it was
now possible to *see* history, or at least a much reduced abstract of it, unfold.
The process of unfolding, however, itself took place in time, and thus sacrificed, as noted earlier, the capacity of the single still image to convey its content immediately – a sacrifice Priestley tried to avoid by creating his chart,
published in 1765, as a very large single folded sheet which, when unfolded,
could be hung on a wall.[38] In Priestley's own words in the *Description of a
Chart of Biography* (Warrington, 1764), "This Chart, which is about three feet
in length, and two feet in breadth, represents the interval of time between
the year 1200 before the Christian era and 1800 after Christ, divided by an
equal scale into centuries. It contains about two thousand names of persons
the most distinguished in the annals of fame, the length of whose lives is
here represented by lines drawn in proportion to their real duration, and ter-
minated in such a manner as to correspond to the dates of their births and
deaths in universal time."

---

[37]Following tradition, time is divided into three epochs: from the creation of the earth to the
founding of Rome, from the founding of Rome to the birth of Christ, and from the birth of
Christ to the author's own time.

[38]For convenience and perhaps to reduce the price, publishers also made the Chart of Biography (76x108 cms.) available in separate sheets devoted to particular professions and particular time periods. Sold as a portfolio of charts, these had to be viewed in succession and thus,
like Dubourg's *Carte*, sacrificed simultaneity. One such version was put out by the Philadelphia publisher M. Carey in 1803, nine years after Priestley settled in Pennsylvania and a year
before his death.

Like Dubourg, Priestley—also a good friend of Franklin—was motivated by the desire to popularize knowledge and so help to create an informed public capable of sound judgment and wise action. And like Dubourg (who had translated Bolingbroke's *Letters on the Study and Use of History*), Priestley believed that history was an essential instrument of civic education. In particular, it seems, Priestley was interested in pointing out some significant lessons that could be derived from his celebrated and immensely popular *Chart of Biography*[39] [figs. 71–73]. Where Dubourg inscribed only the name at the point of birth in his *Carte Chronologique*, Priestley inscribed a full lifeline extending horizontally over the appropriate time period for each of his entries, The bunching of biographical lifelines in the vertically ordered sections devoted to artists, scientists, and men of learning ("Mathematicians, etc., Physicians," "Artists, Poets," and to a lesser extent "Orators, Critics, etc." and "Historians, Antiquaries, Lawyers" in Priestley's own categorization), is immediately visible to the eye in contrast to the relatively constant number of lifelines in the sections devoted to "Statesmen and Warriors" or "Divines, and Metaphysicians"—considerably more so, of course, in the single sheet version than in the cheaper and more common book version—as it moves from left to right along the horizontal timeline, which Priestley divided evenly by century (though he also inscribed the uneven succession of reigning monarchs, from Saul to George III, along with the regular succession of centuries, at the bottom of his chart). This bunching up of scientists, men of letters, and artists demonstrated vividly, according to Priestley, that "civilization," the part of history created by productive and peace-loving men and women, was "progressing," that learning builds on learning, and that the pace of progress quickens as the numbers of men of learning, poets, and artists increase and communication among them becomes more intense. Priestley was thus directing the attention of the viewer of his chart to a particular relationship revealed in it.[40] That relationship might also have been expressed even more immediately, if more abstractly, as a graph, in which one line representing notable warriors and statesmen would have started off fairly high on a vertical numerical scale but would have risen quite slowly as it advanced from century to century on the horizontal time scale. Other lines representing notable artists, scientists, and men of learning would have started off low on the vertical numerical scale but moved upward at an ever-increasing pace as they advanced from left to right on the horizontal timeline until at some point they intersected the line of statesmen and warriors and then rose quite steeply above it.

---

[39]On possible reasons for the relatively slight impact of Dubourg's *Carte* compared with Priestley's *Chart*, see Ferguson, "The 1753 *Carte chronographique*," pp. 217–18.

[40]On Priestley's chart, see Rosenberg, "Joseph Priestly and the Graphic Invention of Modern Time," pp. 55–103. Unfortunately, the images in the accompanying online image portfolio were taken not from the now rare single sheet version of the Chart of Biography (a copy of which can be seen in the Rare Book Room at Princeton University's Firestone Library) but from the portfolio version put out by the Philadelphia publisher M. Carey in 1803.

III

Enlightenment and Growing
Interest in Statistics

The Enlightenment approach to history and the study of the past made such a graphic representation of historical data and historical change both likely and desirable. First, there was a shift of emphasis from the *gesta* of the great and powerful to the day-to-day living conditions of the humble (as reflected, for instance, in the relation of wages to the cost of food, clothing, and shelter, and in mortality rates and expectation of life at various ages), from politics and wars to commerce, industry, and the arts, from the dramatic history of "eagles and vultures tearing each other to pieces" overhead, in the words of Voltaire, to the peaceful, purposeful, invisible history of "ants silently digging out dwelling-places for themselves" beneath the surface of things—that is, in other words, from eminently narratable historiographical material with well-defined individual heroes and actions to commonplace, generic, infinitely repeated actions and events that can be considered in abstraction from their uniqueness and that do not lend themselves so readily to traditional narrative, but in compensation, thanks to their relative homogeneity, can be measured and quantitatively compared.[41] Second, history was now expected to be *useful,* not only by presenting moral and civic lessons but by contributing to human well-being in practical ways.

Traditionally a branch of literature, history was already beginning to be reconceived as a "social science." By asking specific questions of the past and using precise historical data (albeit data abstracted from the rich texture of life) to establish correlations, many Enlightenment scholars believed men of learning should be able to develop a "science" of society and to propose policies and design institutions that would benefit humanity. That was the goal pursued by both Adam Smith and Thomas Malthus, the latter's pessimism notwithstanding. If enlightened rulers increasingly gathered statistics

---

[41]Voltaire, *Essai sur les moeurs*, ch. 81, in *Oeuvres complètes*, ed. Louis Moland (Paris: Garnier, 1877–85), vol. 12, pp. 53–54.

in order to better control their realms, enlightened men of learning turned to statistics—and to what they could learn from historical statistics, from statistical patterns over time—in order to construct a "scientific" understanding of the human world, and come up with effective ways of improving it. The son of Sir John Sinclair, the initiator and editor of the celebrated twenty-one-volume *Statistical Account of Scotland* (Edinburgh, 1791), explained that though his father "had derived the term [statistics] from the German, [. . .] he employed it in a sense somewhat different from its foreign acceptation." For "in Germany, a statistical inquiry related to the *political strength* of the country, or to questions of state policy, whereas he employed the word to express an inquiry into the state of a country, for the purpose of ascertaining the amount of *happiness* enjoyed by its inhabitants, and the means of its future improvement."[42]

Even though the pioneering demographic research of John Graunt and Gregory King in the seventeenth century,[43] like that of Johann Peter Süssmilch in Germany in the eighteenth, is probably to be seen as serving the ends of the state rather than those of humanity as a whole, the language of public utility was used to justify their work. "Finding some *Truths*, and not commonly believed Opinions, to arise from my Meditations upon these neglected *Papers* [i.e. the bills of mortality]," Graunt announced in the Preface to his classic *Natural and Political Observations . . . made upon the Bills of Mortality* (London, 1662), "I proceeded farther, to consider what benefit the knowledge of the same would bring to the World."

Along with demography, the first decade of the eighteenth century saw the opening of another new field of historical research: the history of prices. In answer to an inquiry from an Oxford scholar as to whether "a Fellow who has an Estate in Land of Inheritance, or a perpetual Pension of Five Pounds per Annum, may conscientiously keep his Fellowship and ought not to be compelled to leave the same, tho' the Statutes of his College did then vacate his Fellowship on such Condition," William Fleetwood, Bishop of St. Asaph

---

[42]*Memoirs of the Life and Works of Sir John Sinclair, Bart. by his son, the Rev. John Sinclair, M.A.* (Edinburgh: William Blackwood; London: T. Cadell, 1837), 2 vols., vol. 1, pp. 9–10. Interest in statistics in France (along with introduction of the term) dates, characteristically, from the Napoleonic period; see Jean-Claude Perrot, "La Statistique dans le premier dictionnaire d'économie politique en langue française," in *Une Histoire intellectuelle de l'économie politique (XVII-XVIII siècle)* (Paris: Editions de l'Ecole des Hautes Etudes en Sciences Sociales, 1992), pp. 127–42.

[43]Graunt (1620–1674) utilized data gathered from bills of mortality stretching back many decades to determine the most common causes of death, identify endemic diseases, establish the ratio of male births to female births, compare the life expectancy of both sexes, and calculate life expectancy at different ages. In his *Natural and Political Observations and Conclusions upon the State and Condition of England,* King (1648–1712) estimates the population and wealth of England at the close of the 17th century, describes the demographic characteristics of the population of England and Wales (age, gender, marital status, numbers of children, servants and dependents), calculates the amount of beer, ale, and malt consumed annually (estimates based on intelligent inferences from data made available through tax records), and speculates on present and future levels of world population. *Of the Naval Trade of England, 1688, and the National Profit then Arising thereby* (written 1697) offers a statistical summary of the trade and wealth of England from 1600 to 1688.

and Bishop of Ely and a product of Eton and Cambridge, replied in the affirmative. He did so on the basis of "the *Decrease* of the *Value of Money* and [. . .] the *Increase* of the *Value of Corn* and other *Commodities, Etc.*" since the time (between 1440 and 1460) when the statutes of the college were promulgated. The scholar may keep his fellowship, he claimed, because even though he now has an income of "VI Pounds *per An.* as Money and Things go *now* [. . .] VI l[ibri] *now* is not worth what V l[ibri] was *then*, when that Statute was first made."

In order to answer the Oxford scholar's question, Fleetwood first undertook to ascertain what the value of £5 in 1440s money would be in 1707; in other words, what sum of money in 1707 would have purchasing power equivalent to £5 in 1440. (He figured it was about £28 or £30.) The outcome of his research into this question, published in his *Chronicon Preciosum* (1707),[44] was hundreds of pages of tables, listing somewhat haphazardly the changing prices of basic items of food, drink, and clothing over the 350-year-period from 1440 to 1707 as well as the wages of various kinds of laborers over the same period [figs. 74, 75]. A highly original, if in some respects (the listing of sources, for instance) rather slapdash piece of historical research into the changing purchasing power of labor had thus been undertaken for an end that was certainly practical and utilitarian, albeit not very different in its original motivation from the historical researches that had long been undertaken by lawyers and antiquarians to settle countless disputes over rights, privileges, and ownership of land.

Four decades after Fleetwood's *Chronicon* the French scholar, antiquarian, translator of Milton, and royal councillor Nicolas-François Dupré de Saint-Maur published an *Essai sur les Monnoies ou Réflexions sur le rapport entre l'argent et les denrées* (Paris: Coignard et De Bure, 1746), in which he presented in tabular form over many pages both the variations in the value of the coinage from 1288 until 1746 (in the first essay) and the changing prices of major items of food, clothing, and—very occasionally—labor, between 1202 and 1742 (in the second essay) [figs. 76, 77]. The selection of items listed under any one year was dependent on the sources available to the author and was therefore inevitably somewhat haphazard. The heterogeneity of the data was aggravated by the difficulty—to which Dupré refers frequently in both the notes and the text—of reconciling the many systems of weights and measures prevailing in different parts of the country and taking account of the influence of particular local conditions (average weather here, drought there; conditions of peace here, war or social unrest there).[45]

---

[44]Full title: *Chronicon Preciosum, or An Account of English Money, the Price of Corn, and other Commodities, for the last 600 Years. In a Letter to a Student at the University of Oxford* (London: Charles Harper). The title of the 1745 edition (London: T. Osborne) was slightly different: *Chronicon Preciosum, or An Account of English Gold and Silver Money; The Price of Corn and other Commodities; and of Stipends, Salaries, Wages, Jointures, Portions, Day-labour, &c. in England for Six hundred Years last past.*

[45]Even in war conditions, Dupré observes, local differences are significant. Thus the price at which a farmer, menaced by approaching armies, can sell his crop will go down, whereas the cost of the same product in a town preparing to withstand a siege will go up.

Still, an effort was made to extrapolate from the mass of data in order to establish a "normal" or "natural" ratio between the price of wheat and the price of oats (pp. 181–82) and to link deviations from that norm to unsettling events in political life or to natural calamities. History could thus be seen "taking shape" in relation to the baseline of a fixed natural order.[46]

By the second half of the century the kind of historically oriented inquiry pioneered by Graunt, Fleetwood, and Dupré, among others, was being harnessed to the Enlightenment project of improving the life of all humanity through an empirically based science of society. Thus Adam Smith made use of the tables of Fleetwood and Dupré in Book I, chapter XI of *The Wealth of Nations* (1776).[47] In the last decade of the century a work appeared in which a vast array of historical statistics documenting the living conditions of the "labouring classes" over many centuries was brought to bear on the continuing problem of the poor. An appendix of over 100 pages in Sir Frederick Morton Eden's remarkable *The State of the Poor, or a history of the labouring classes in England, from the Conquest to the present period; in which are particularly considered, their domestic economy, with respect to diet, dress, fuel, and habitation; and the various plans which, from time to time, have been proposed and adopted for the relief of the poor* (3 vols., London: B. & J. White; G. G. & J. Robinson; T. Payne; R. Faulder; T. Egerton; J. Debrett; and D. Bremner, 1797), consists of an exhaustive

---

[46]"Toutes les fois que dans un espace de temps déterminé, le setier d'avoine, mesure de Paris, s'est vendu à peu près un tiers de moins que le setier de blé, les choses étoient dans leur ordre naturel.

"Lorque notre setier d'avoine s'est vendu la moitié moins ou plus désavantageusement, il est palpable qu'il y a eu quelque calamité causée par les accidens naturels, ou par les guerres, & la famine étoit d'autant plus grande, que l'avoine se trouvoit plus au-dessous du blé.

"Depuis 1596 jusques vers l'an 1635, le prix de l'avoine n'alloit guères qu'à la moitié de celle du blé. Dans les années qui suivent, le prix de l'avoine monte environ de deux tiers de celui du froment. La disproportion entre le premier & le dernier prix de ces grains, étoit l'ouvrage des guerres civiles de Religion." (p. 182)

A general reduction in the price of cereals is attributed "probablement" to "le calme dont nous jouissons dans l'intérieur du Royaume depuis cent cinquante ans." (p. 182)

[47]In *The Wealth of Nations*, Book I, ch. XI (Modern Library ed., 1937, p. 198), Smith refers respectfully to "three very faithful, diligent, and laborious collectors of the prices of corn, Mr. Dupré de St. Maur, Mr. Messance [*Recherches sur la population des généralités d'Auvergne, de Lyon, de Rouen, et de quelques provinces et villes du royaume, avec des réflexions sur la valeur du bled tant en France qu'en Angleterre, depuis 1674 jusqu'en 1764, par M. Messance, receveur des tailles de l'élection de Saint-Etienne* (Paris, 1766)], and the author of the Essay on the police of grain [C. J. Herbert, *Essai sur la police générale des grains, sur leur prix et sur les effets de l'agriculture* (Londres, 1753)]." To these works was added in a letter of 15 January 1769 to Lord Hailes (Sir David Dalrymple, an Edinburgh lawyer, antiquary and man of letters) Charles Smith's *Three Tracts on the Corn Trade and Corn Laws* (London, 1766); see *Correspondence of Adam Smith*, ed. Ernest Campbell Mossner and Ian Simpson Ross (Oxford University Press, revised ed., 1987; The Glasgow Edition of the Works and Correspondence of Adam Smith, vol. 6), p. 139. All four books, along with Fleetwood, were in Smith's personal library. Starting from the physiocratic premise that agriculture is the foundation of the wealth of nations, Herbert argues—using historical evidence—for the lifting of restrictions on the corn trade in France. Messance's *Recherches* contain many tables of population statistics over the previous century or so and a smaller number presenting comparisons of grain prices in various markets over a similar period.

table in which are aligned in three parallel columns, for every three or four years from 1125 until 1619, the "Price of Provisions" (i.e. of various qualities and quantities of wheat, oats, barley, rye, malt, peas, beans, eggs, butter, milk, cream, etc.; of an ox, a cow, a sheep, a lamb, a goose, a swan, a duck, etc.; of veal, pork, and beef; of sugar, salt, pepper and other spices, artichokes, almonds, etc.; of various kinds of beer, wine, and other drinks); the "Price of other Commodities" (e.g. green cloth, scarlet cloth, linen, a sack of wool, a strong horse, a cart-horse, a horse and cart), and the "Price of Labour" (e.g. the wages of a harvest man, a footman, a thresher, a baker, a miller, a shepherd, a mason, a carpenter, a plumber, "a manservant in husbandry of the best sort," "a common servant who can mow"; the labor cost of "spreading dung on four acres of inclosed land," of "threshing and dressing one quarter of rye," etc.) [figs. 78–81]. This table, extending over sixty quarto pages, is complemented by a further forty pages containing shorter tables of comparative prices and wages over the period from 1229 to 1796.[48]

The historical interest and utility of this amazing compilation is clearly explained by the author:

> The Annalist, who wishes to inform, must often quit the splendid scenes of national glory, and condescend to particularize the humbler occupations of mankind. Hume is, perhaps, the only one of our modern historians, who has justly appreciated the value of information, which, before his time, had been usually deemed frivolous and unimportant; but which, attentively considered, [. . .] solves the important question;—whether the condition of society is retrograde, stationary, or progressive. Thus, I conceive, a chronological account of the prices of labour and of commodities, (however lightly some may esteem such objects of enquiry,) would alone, (when it could be procured,) furnish a complete epitome of the most important

---

[48]One lists the annual prices of wheat and malt, derived from the audit-books of Eton College, at the market in Windsor from 1595 to 1796; another the prices of "Grains and Coals in London during the last 65 years." A "Comparative Table of the Prices of Mutton and Wool" lists prices every few years from 1229 to 1724, then annually until 1760. A "Comparative Table of the Prices of Wool" at different markets covers the period from 1761 to 1795. A table of the annual prices of beef, pork, butter, and two different kinds of cheese is based on the account-books of the "Victualling Office" of the Royal Navy between 1740 and 1795. (As is his custom, Eden is careful to draw attention to the particular character of these last data. They reflect the prices paid by a government procurement agency. Hence "These prices are considerably lower than the price paid by the consumer; which, in 1795 was about 7d. a pound for beef and mutton." The data remain valuable, however, in that "they shew [. . .] the proportion between the prices of different periods."). Yet another table lists the annual number of cattle and sheep slaughtered and sold at Smithfield Market in London between 1732 and 1794, showing that it increased irregularly but quite spectacularly over the 60-year period—a sign, in Eden's view, of increasing prosperity. Finally, several tables, based on statutes or other documents dated 1495, 1593 and 1610, provide an account of the wages set or actually paid for many different kinds of labor.

branch of history; for it would enable us to judge, what quantities of the necessaries and conveniences of life equal portions of labour have procured at different periods; or, in other words, to determine, whether the great business of human life has been conducted with more or less facility.[49]

Though he takes great care to point out the difficulties the historian faces in interpreting the statistical data available to him,[50] there is no doubt in Eden's mind about the importance or value of the goal. It is to ascertain which conditions have been "most favorable to industry" (p. vii)—by which he obviously means "industriousness" rather than what we now understand by "industry"—in order, presumably, to promote such conditions on as broad a national and indeed international scale as possible.

As the example of Eden shows and as the work of Smith and other economists (and later of Marx) also demonstrates, historical statistics played a significant role in the new social "sciences." Understanding the present and improving present conditions, it was believed, required not only statistical data about the present but also statistical data about the past. From an analysis of all the data it might be possible to derive the "laws" and processes of

---

[49]Appendix I, p. iii.

[50]Just as he meticulously cites the sources of his information—in deliberate contrast to the earlier work of Fleetwood—Eden warns his reader that "Tables of Prices are not altogether free from several objections, which ought to render us extremely cautious in drawing conclusions from any single, although well authenticated, fact. The accounts, for instance, of the prices of grain, are in general only those, which from the particular circumstances of the time, attracted the attention of the Annalist: they are usually the prices in dearths and famines, or in years of extraordinary cheapness; and are therefore no very accurate criterion of the mean or ordinary price: it is often impossible to ascertain the capacity of the measures that were used, or to point out the places where the prices were taken. In the distracted state of the country from the twelfth to the fifteenth century, the intercourse between the different parts of the island was interrupted: the want of good roads, an injudicious system of agriculture, and the desolating incursions of rival barons, often prevented one part of the kingdom, where the crop was scanty, from being supplied with the superabundant produce of another.[. . .] In some instances it is difficult to distinguish, whether the rent of land, as stated in ancient records, is the whole benefit the landlord received, or whether the personal services of the tenant did not constitute by far the most valuable part; in others, whether the price of grain is the price for which it sold in the market, or the quota which, in ancient times, tenants paid to their landlords in lieu of a rent in kind, and which was always much below the market price." (p. v) Any conclusion we might draw about "the condition of that class, which lives by wages" is therefore "only true with regard to the same time and place. A comparison of the earnings in London with the price of provisions in Scotland, or of the price of labour in London at the Revolution with the price of the necessaries of life at the same place in 1796, will not ascertain, which country, or which period, has been most favourable to industry." (p.vii) In accordance with the best Enlightenment practice since Bayle and Bierling, Eden considers that the data "most entitled to credit" are those "which are incidentally mentioned by writers, without any view to establish a favourite position." Thus, for example, "William Thorn's account of the bill of fare, and of the prices of many of the articles consumed at Ralph de Bourne's installation feast in 1309, may perhaps be depended on; because (as Adam Smith observes,) they are not recorded on account of their extraordinary dearness, or cheapness; but are mentioned incidentally as the prices actually paid for large quantities of grain consumed at a feast which was famous for its magnificence." (p. vi)

social life; these, in turn, would make it possible to develop intelligent measures for the improvement of the human condition.

The tables in Fleetwood, Dupré, and Eden took up many pages. Neither the connections between different statistical series (such as prices and wages) nor the trends, if any, of the series themselves were easily discernible.[51] This drawback was aggravated by the heterogeneity of the data provided in the tables. It was thus a major step forward when William Playfair, a compatriot and younger contemporary of Adam Smith, came up with a means of graphically representing not only statistical data about specific conditions at any one time but changes in the data over time. Thanks to Playfair, it was now possible at a single glance to perceive the character, velocity, and direction of change, as well as changes in the relations among different historical series. As Playfair himelf explained,

> Having been requested by the English editor of Mr. Boetticher's statistical Tables, to consider some method of bringing them down to [the present] period, without injuring the original work, I proposed to make a supplementary table, comprehending all the countries which have undergone any material change since the publication of the book. [. . .] In the course of executing that design, it occurred to me, that tables are by no means a good form for conveying such information. [. . .] Making an appeal to the eye when proportion and magnitude are concerned, is the best and readiest method of conveying a distinct idea.

Playfair also made it clear that his method is best adapted to a different kind of material from that which constitutes the matter of most traditional historical narratives. "The numbers of people, quantity of ground, revenues, prices of labour, &c. as simple and useful facts, belong to statistics; but the description of the order of the garter, or of the golden fleece, has nothing to do with it."[52]

With Playfair's invention of the flow chart, the bar chart, and the pie chart in the closing decades of the eighteenth century, historiography

---

[51]Christiaan Huyghens had, however, responded in letters dated 21 and 28 November 1669 to a letter from his brother Lodewijk containing data on life expectancy taken from Graunt's *Natural and Political Observations on the Bills of Mortality* of 1662 by designing a curve that showed how many people out of a hundred survive between infancy and the age of 86. See the reproduction of this curve in Howard Wainer, *Graphic Discovery. A Trout in the Milk and Other Visual Adventures* (Princeton: Princeton University Press, 2005), p. 13.

[52]*The Statistical Breviary; Shewing, on a Principle Entirely New, the Resources of Every State and Kingdom in Europe* (London: T. Bensley, 1801), Preface, p. 4, in William Playfair, *The Commercial and Political Atlas and Statistical Breviary*, ed. Howard Wainer and Ian Spence (Cambridge: Cambridge University Press, 2000). The work Playfair was asked to update was Jakob Gottlieb Boetticher, *Übersicht-Tabellen aller europäischen Staaten nebst deren Münzen. Maassen und Gewichten* (Königsberg: Hartung, 1789).

acquired a form of visual illustration appropriate to its new concern with "the humbler occupations of mankind" rather than "the splendid scenes of national glory."[53] The flow chart, in particular, was admirably suited to represent change over time in a single, immediately viewable image.

---

[53] It is not surprising that the inventor of the flow chart, the bar chart, and the pie chart, was an Enlightenment Scotsman. "Il y a lieu de croire," the author of an anonymous 12-page pamphlet (*Observations sur les statistiques de l'Ecosse* [Brussels: Imprimerie Mailly, 1815], p. 1) wrote about the celebrated 21-volume *Statistical Account of Scotland* (Edinburgh, 1791–98) initiated, designed, and edited by Sir John Sinclair, that in Scotland "les recherches de nature statistique ont été faites avec une plus grande attention minutieuse, et ont été portées à un plus haut degré de perfection que dans aucune autre partie de l'Europe." Sinclair's *Statistical Account* was more complete than any other similar work. "Aucun autre pays de l'Europe ne possède un pareil document."

IV

William Playfair and the Invention of Modern Graphics

Though historiography, as we shall see, was in fact slow to avail itself of the new resource, the flow chart, the bar chart, and the pie chart are now ubiquitous features of modern historiographical writing. They are also in everyday use in countless other contexts, including daily newspapers. Yet their inventor is virtually unknown. A few words about him will therefore not be out of place. Born in 1759 in a village near the East Coast Scottish town of Dundee, William Playfair received his early education from his father, the local Presbyterian minister, and after the latter's death in 1771, from his then 24-year-old brother John, who was later to be Dugald Stewart's successor in the chair of mathematics at the University of Edinburgh and one of Britain's foremost mathematicians and scientists.[54] At the age of fourteen, he was apprenticed to Andrew Meikle (1719–1811), the inventor of the threshing machine,[55] and three years later was recommended by the Rev. Robert Small, a friend and colleague of his father, for the position of draughtsman and assistant to the great Scottish engineer, James Watt, who had not long before opened his steam engine factory in Birmingham in partnership with Matthew Bolton. Through the good offices of Robert Small's

---

[54]In addition to his work in mathematics, John Playfair helped to popularize the principle of uniformitarianism of his colleague and friend, the Edinburgh geologist James Hutton. It was through John Playfair's *Illustrations of the Huttonian Theory of the Earth* (1802) that Hutton's ideas reached Charles Lyell, who developed them further in his influential *Principles of Geology* (1830–33). Through the tutoring of John, William may well have bcome familiar with various diagrammatic schemes devised by Leibniz and Euler, and before them, Giordano Bruno and Ramòn Lull, to illustrate logical propositions. See the essential article by Ian Spence, "No Humble Pie: The Origin and Use of a Statistical Chart," *Journal of Educational and Behavioral Statistics*, 30 (2005): 353-68.

[55]Meikle himself was in the employ of the Rennie family on their estate not far from Edinburgh. The fourth son of the family, Playfair's fellow engineer-in-training, subsequently achieved renown as the builder of bridges and docks throughout Britain, including, in London alone, Waterloo Bridge, Southwark Bridge, London Bridge, and the West India docks.

brother, Dr. William Small, a graduate of Marischal College, Aberdeen, and from 1758 until 1764 professor of mathematics at the College of William and Mary in Virginia—where he had been Thomas Jefferson's most important mentor[56]—Playfair became acquainted in Birmingham with several members of the Lunar Society, of which Small, on his return to Britain, had been one of the founders.[57] Among the members of the Lunar Society were Erasmus Darwin, Watt, Josiah Wedgwood—and Joseph Priestley. It was Priestley's famous biographical chart (described earlier) that, according to Playfair himself, was the inspiration for his own path-breaking economic and political charts.[58]

Though he revered Watt, Playfair left his position with him in 1782 to embark on a colorful career as—in the words of Ian Spence and Howard Wainer, the two modern scholars to whom we owe what knowledge we have of the inventor of the now ubiquitous flow, bar, and pie charts—"in turn [. . .] accountant, inventor, silversmith, merchant, investment broker, economist, statistician, pamphleteer, translator, publicist, land speculator, convict, banker, ardent royalist, editor [of Smith's *The Wealth of Nations*], blackmailer, and journalist." According to Spence and Wainer, "some of [Playfair's] business activities were questionable, if not downright illegal, and it may fairly be said that he was something of a rogue and scoundrel."[59] Having moved to Paris in 1787, Playfair engaged not only in a number of— mostly unsuccessful—business ventures but also in the storming of the Bastille in 1789. However, the excesses of the Jacobins and a murky scheme in which he was accused of embezzlement and threatened with incarceration led him to quickly leave France in 1791. In the various journalistic and publishing ventures in which he engaged after his return to Britain he proved to be a fierce critic of the Revolution. After the Restoration, however, he wrote a pamphlet advocating France as a more promising destination for enterprising emigrants from Britain than the usual overseas destinations.[60]

In 1786 Playfair published his groundbreaking *Commercial and Political Atlas; Representing, by Means of Stained Copper-Plate Charts, the Exports,*

[56]See William Playfair, *The Commercial and Political Atlas and Statistical Breviary*, ed. Howard Wainer and Ian Spence, Introduction, pp. 3–4.

[57]G. Hull, "William Small 1734–1775: no publications, much influence," *Journal of the Royal Society of Medicine*, 90 (February 1997): 102–05. It was thanks to a letter of introduction from Benjamin Franklin that Small made the acquaintance of Matthew Bolton and his circle of friends in Birmingham, the nucleus of the Lunar Society.

[58]"The study of chronology has been much facilitated by making space represent time, and a line of proportional length, and in a suitable position, the life of a man, by means of which the remarkable men of past ages appear as it were before us in their proper time and place. The author of this work applied the use of lines to matters of commerce and finance about fifteen years ago." A note names the work of "fifteen years ago" to which the author applied Priestley's use of lines as "the Political and Commercial Atlas, delineating the progress of the commerce and revenues of this country during the last century." (William Playfair, *The Statistical Breviary* [London: T. Bensley, 1801], p. 15).

[59]Ian Spence and Howard Wainer, "Visual Revelations," *Chance*, 10 (1997): 35–37.

[60]*The Advantages of Emigration to France Clearly Shewn to be Infinitely Superior to All Others* (London: John Souter, n.d.)

Imports, and General Trade of England; the National Debt, and other Public Accounts; with Observations and Remarks (London: J Debrett; Edinburgh: W. Creech and C. Elliot; Dublin: L. White).[61] Though modeled on a geographical atlas, it contained no maps, only statistical charts along with tables of the data on which these were based. (The tables had been included at the urging of Watt, who was concerned, in the interests of accuracy and credibility, that sources and exact figures should be provided; they were retained in the second edition of 1787, but omitted, as Playfair became more self-confident, from the third edition of 1801.)[62] A French translation appeared in 1787, a copy of which was presented to Louis XVI and apparently elicited warm praise from the monarch, an amateur geographer.[63]

The first edition was printed in folio (216 x 330 mm), with the type set in landscape format rather than the usual portrait format in order to accommodate charts that would have been far less effective if they had been forced into the vertical format. By the third edition (1801), however, the conventional vertical format was adopted for the text, though only two of the charts were printed in that format (20 and 21). Most were printed in landscape format, requiring the reader to hold the book at right angles in order to read them. Two (1 and 19) which were double or three times the page size, were printed as foldouts. The charts presented the shifting pattern of England's exports and imports and of the balance of trade (favorable or unfavorable) in the country's commerce with all the major countries of Europe, Russia, Africa, the East and West Indies, Bermuda, North America, Greenland, Ireland, and the Channel Islands from 1700 to 1800 or, as the title of the third edition stated clearly, *The Progress of the Commerce, Revenues, Expenditure, and Debts of England during the Whole of the Eighteenth Century*. Additional charts offered a comparative view of the "Annual Revenues of England and France from the middle of the 16th century to the end of the 18th," a view of the development of "the National Debt of England from the Revolution [1688] to the end of the War with America," expenditures on the Royal Navy and on the army in the course of the eighteenth century, and similar matters. Most of the charts plot pounds sterling on the ordinate against time on the abscissa [figs., XII*, XIII*, XIV*, XV*. 83–88, 90-92, 95]. Only one chart, which, in the absence of sufficient data for other years, plotted the value of Scotland's imports from and

---

[61]The slightly amended title of the 1787 edition carried the important additional words "*at a single View*."

[62]Responding to a prepublication version Playfair circulated among his friends, Watt wrote (10 October 1785): "I can think of nothing in addition to your plan, except that it might be proper to give in letter press the Tables from which the Charts have been constructed [. . .], for the charts now seem to rest on your own authority and it will naturally be enquired from whence you have derived your intelligence." (Quoted in *The Commercial and Political Atlas and Statistical Breviary*, ed. Howard Wainer and Ian Spence, Introduction, p. 14) Even after he dropped accompanying tables, Playfair did sometimes indicate where the data supporting a chart were weak, as in a comment on Plate 19 of *The Commercial and Political Atlas*.

[63]Playfair's "Introduction" to the *Commercial and Political Atlas*, 3rd ed., p. ix, note, in *The Commercial and Political Atlas and Statistical Breviary*, ed. Howard Wainer and Ian Spence.

exports to seventeen different European countries and other parts of the world in the single year from Christmas 1780 to Christmas 1781, did not include time as a dimension. In this respect it resembled a map or a still image rather than a narrative or moving picture. Because it did "not comprehend any portion of time," however, this first known case of the now-common bar chart was considered by Playfair "much inferior in utility to those that do"[64] and it was dropped from the 1801 edition [fig. 89]. Nevertheless, the bar chart had a considerable future ahead of it, in historical writing as well as in sociology and economics, not only as a convenient and effective way of representing the results of a synchronic cut through different but comparable data at a given moment in time but, when arranged in series, as a way of delineating change.

The graphics in the three editions of Playfair's *Atlas*[65] are strikingly similar to those still in use today. As Wainer and Spence put it: "hachure, shading, color coding, and grids with major and minor divisions were all introduced in the various editions of the *Atlas*. Actual, missing, and hypothetical data were portrayed, and the kind of line used, solid or broken, differentiated the various forms. Playfair filled the areas between the curves in most of the charts to indicate accumulated or total amounts. All included a descriptive title either outside the frame (as in the first edition) or in an oval in the body of the chart (as in the third edition). The axes were labeled and numbered where the major gridlines intersected the frame."[66]

The third major modern form of graphic representation of data, the pie chart, was introduced by Playfair in *The Statistical Breviary; shewing, on a principle entirely new, the Resources of every State and Kingdom in Europe; Illustrated with stained copper-plate charts, representing the principal powers of each distinct nation with ease and perspicuity* (London: J. Wallis, 1801). Unlike the flow charts in the *Atlas*, the pie charts in this volume do not (and, by their nature, like images or maps, could not) provide a temporal dimension. What they offered was a strikingly vivid comparative view of the European states with respect to physical size, population, and wealth. The only way of introducing a temporal dimension was by juxtaposing two pie charts, each representing a situation at a single given point in time. Of the five fold-out charts inserted at the end of the volume, the first represents the land

---

[64]Quoted from 1786 edition, p. 101, in *The Commercial and Political Atlas and Statistical Breviary*, ed. Howard Wainer and Ian Spence, Introduction, p. 15.

[65]Though there are substantial differences among the three editions (see Wainer and Spence, Introduction, pp. 16–17) the character of the graphs is constant, except for the substitution of hachure and stippling for color in the 1787 edition; see following note.

[66]*The Commercial and Political Atlas and Statistical Breviary*, ed. Howard Wainer and Ian Spence, Introduction, p. 15. Hachure and stippled dots were used in the 1787 edition instead of color, dark colors being indicated by hachure and lighter colors by stippling. Where color was used, as in the hand colored copperplates of the first and third editions, a thick red hand-painted line might be used for exports as in the 1801 edition, a yellow-orange line for imports. A favorable balance of trade might be indicated by a solid blue-green or brownish fill color between the export and import lines, an unfavorable or negative balance by a pink solid fill between the two lines. Color was thus used to highlight both the difference between the two time series (exports and imports) and the difference in the resulting trade balance.

area, number of inhabitants, and revenues (in million of pounds sterling) of each major European country, including Russia and Turkey, just before the French Revolution; the second presents the same information after the Treaty of Lunéville (1801), "which so alters the nature of affairs, and the extent of France and Germany"[67] [figs. 93, 94]. Each country is represented by a circle, or "pie," the relative size and placement of which (the series is aligned on a diminishing scale from left to right) indicates the extent of its land area, which is also marked in numbers in the center of the pie and which is color-coded, green indicating a maritime power, pale red a country powerful only on land. His aim, Playfair explained, was to "aid statistical studies by shewing to the eye the sizes of different countries, represented by similar forms, for where forms are not similar, the eye cannot compare them easily nor accurately. From this circumstance it happens, that we have a more accurate idea of the sizes of the planets, which are spheres, than of the nations of Europe, which we see on maps, all of which are irregular forms in themselves as well as unlike to each other."[68]

In two cases the pie is divided—the Turkish Empire into smaller European and African sections or tranches and a much larger (more than half) Asiatic section, and the Russian Empire into two concentric circles, the thick outer ring representing the extensive "Asiatic Dominions" and the smaller inner ring the "European Dominions." Rising vertically from the left side of each pie, a red line indicates on a population scale, located in the left margin, the number of inhabitants of the country; a yellow line rising vertically from the right side of the pie indicates the revenues of each country in millions of pounds sterling (scale located in the right margin). On the top of each pie—a concession to purely tabular, nonvisual display of information—a number is placed indicating the number of inhabitants per square mile (5 for the Russian Dominions, 14 for Sweden, 67 for Portugal, 174 for France before the Revolution, 257 for the United Provinces or Holland, etc.). A dotted line is drawn in each case between the left red line (the population line) and the right yellow line (the revenue line). Though the angle is inevitably distorted by the thickness (i.e. land area) of the pie, the direction of the line—a sharp upward direction indicating high revenue in relation to population—was intended to indicate relatively lower or relatively higher taxation.

The third pie chart represents, from left to right, the relative populations of European cities that are or once were capitals of countries on a diminishing scale: from London, the largest (1,100,000), by way of Constantinople (900,000), Paris (690,000), Naples (380,000) to Stockholm (63,000) and Edinburgh, the smallest (60,000). The fourth and fifth charts use the same system to provide statistical information about the various parts of "Hindoostan that are connected with, or influence European affairs in the east."

---

[67] *The Statistical Breviary; Shewing, on a Principle Entirely New, the Resources of every State and Kingdom in Europe* (London: J. Wallis, 1801), "Introduction and Explanation of the Statistical Charts," p. 14.

[68] Ibid., p. 15.

Playfair insisted in many places in his work that his charts made no claim to greater accuracy than tables. Their purpose was to make large amounts of information about social, political, and economic phenomena and the relations among them—as long as these could be expressed in quantitative terms—more immediately perceptible and readily assimilable than would be the case with tables, especially where the information to be conveyed included change over time.

> The advantage proposed by this method, is not that of giving a more accurate statement than by figures [i.e. numbers and tables], but it is to give a more simple and permanent idea of the gradual progress and comparative amounts, at different periods, by presenting to the eye a figure, the proportions of which correspond with the amount of the sums intended to be expressed. [. . .]
>
> Figures and letters may express with accuracy, but they can never *represent* either number or space.[69]
>
> The advantages proposed by this mode of representation, are to facilitate the attainment of information, and aid the memory in retaining it. [. . .] Of all the senses, the eye gives the liveliest and most accurate idea of whatever is susceptible of being represented to it; and when the proportion between different quantities is the object, then the eye has an incalculable superiority.[70]

In short, the chief advantage of his method of "lineal arithmetic" over tables of words and numbers consists, according to Playfair, in making *"time, proportion,* and *amount"* immediately and simultaneously apprehensible by the eye. Tables are not in fact banished from his works. The two principal charts in the *Statistical Breviary,* for instance, are followed by pages of detailed tables containing data about each of the countries represented on the charts, much of it in addition to what is communicated in the charts.[71] The enormous advantage of the chart is "that it gives one simple and general idea, instead of a number of separate ones, and gives form and shape to what otherwise is an abstract idea." In a later work, *A Letter on our*

---

[69]Playfair's "Introduction" to the *Commercial and Political Atlas,* 3rd ed., pp. ix-x, xiii, in *The Commercial and Political Atlas and Statistical Breviary,* ed. Howard Wainer and Ian Spence.

[70]*The Statistical Breviary; Shewing, on a Principle Entirely New, the Resources of every State and Kingdom in Europe* (London: J. Wallis, 1801), "Introduction and Explanation of the Statistical Charts," p. 14.

[71]See likewise the highly detailed table of Russian products exported from Petersburg to Great Britain from 1753 to 1804 in Playfair's *European Commerce, shewing new and secure channels of trade with the continent of Europe: detailing the produce, manufactures, and commerce, of Russia, Prussia, Sweden, Denmark and Germany; as well as the trade of the rivers Elbe, Weser, and Ems; with a general view of the trade, navigation, produce, and manufactures, of the United Kingdom of Great Britain and Ireland; and its unexplored and improvable resources and interior wealth.* (London: J. and J. Richardson, 1805), p. 122.

Agricultural Distresses, their Causes and Remedies (1821), Playfair illustrates his point with a boldly chosen example.

> Nothing can better prove the superiority of charts delineating the rises and falls of prices, and giving one view of the whole over printed tables [. . .] than the following fact:
>
> Dr. Adam Smith, whose abilities and acuteness are well known, gives a table of the prices of wheat from 1202 till the year 1774, when his book was written. His printed table corresponds with this chart [i.e. an accompanying foldout chart drawn by Playfair, see figs. XIV*, XV*, 91, 92—L.G.] yet that great man, in a number of instances, seems to think that the wages of labour should be regulated by the price of wheat, rather than by a money price. He does not indeed actually pretend to determine the question, but [. . .] inclines to the regulation of wages according to the price of wheat.
>
> Thus did Dr. Smith reason, with that table in his possession. Now had he looked at the chart, [. . .] he would have seen that the question on which he reasoned so gravely was not one to be entertained for an instant, as not only wages would have sometimes doubled or fallen one half, from one year to another, but that at the present day they would be what they were in the reign of queen Elizabeth, after having been much lower, and sometimes higher since then.
>
> In one word, the regulation so spoken of would be the greatest absurdity possible, if it were practicable, and when a man of real talents and judgment speaks so, it must be because he has not taken a just view of the matter.
>
> Dr. Adam Smith viewed the fluctuation of prices from a printed table, yet evidently did not form the proper conclusion which men of far inferior abilities will form from the linear chart. [. . .]
>
> The reputation of Adam Smith, as a man of great talents, is established throughout the world. I had the honour and pleasure of knowing him personally, and no man can rate his talents higher than I do; it is for this very reason that I seize the opportunity of shewing how much better ordinary men can judge from a *linear chart*, than a man of great genius did from a *printed table*.
>
> 1st. It appears from this chart that a good workman can, with nine days' wages, purchase a quarter of wheat at this time.
>
> 2nd. That in queen Elizabeth's reign it required seventy-three days' wages to purchase a quarter.
>
> 3rd. That in the first thirty years of the reign of George III, wheat was much lower in money-prices than in the reign of Elizabeth.
>
> 4th. That never at any previous period was the price of wheat so low as in the first thirty years of the last reign.

In addition to demonstrating "the absurdity of regulating the price of labour by the price of wheat," his chart also demonstrates, Playfair adds for good measure, "the fallacy" of the common view that "while gold and silver were the currency of the country, prices were steady, and that the rise of late years was entirely owing to bank notes being used in place of metallic money."[72]

It should be emphasized that Playfair's charts are not simple compendia of information. They are usually designed—as the case just referred to makes plain—to establish a point or convey an argument that tables alone would not convey as vividly or powerfully. The observations (ranging from two to four pages) that follow each chart in the *Commercial and Political Atlas* develop such arguments verbally. Sometimes these are quite specific: for instance, that wars result in a steep rise in the national debt and in the interest payable on it (*Atlas*, 3rd ed., 1801, Charts 19 and 20), or that over-regulation and excessive import and export taxes result in the growth of illicit trade and thus in actual loss, rather than gain, of revenue to the state (Chart 6). Sometimes larger arguments are developed, as in the critiques of government policy toward the American colonies in the observations following Chart 5, of the slave trade and slave labor in general in the observations following Chart 16, or of the East India Company in the observations following Chart 3. The "Remarks and General Observations" following the first chart in the *Atlas*, the subject of which is the overall pattern of English exports and imports from 1700 to 1800, anticipate the central theme of the author's later *Inquiry into the Permanent Causes of the Decline and Fall of Powerful and Wealthy Nations [. . .] designed to shew how the Prosperity of the British Empire may be Prolonged* (London: Greenland and Norris, 1805; 2nd ed., 1807). The chart shows that the volume and value of England's trade increased over the entire period. But it also shows a progressively diminishing positive balance of trade from mid-century on, with, in addition, a fairly sharp downturn in volume and even a brief crossover into a negative trade balance in the decade from 1770 to 1780 [figs. XII*, 82]. Playfair interprets this as follows—in the sense of the French saying that "il est plus facile de devenir riche que de le rester":

> From the beginning of the century till the year 1750, our exports regularly increased faster than our imports, so that the balance in favour of this country was greater than it had ever been before; but, from that time, though our commerce has upon the whole doubled in its amount, yet the balance in our favour is not equal to what it was then: this is a proof that luxury has greatly increased amongst us; and, not only increased, but that it has done so beyond even the proportion of our extended commerce.

---

[72]William Playfair, *A Letter on our Agricultural Distresses, their Causes and Remedies, accompanied with Tables and Copper-Plate Charts, shewing and comparing the Prices of Wheat, Bread, and Labour from 1565 to 1821* (London: William Sams, 1821), Appendix C, pp. 44–47.

The trade of this country received a great blow in the years 1771, 1772, by the failure of some great merchantile houses, which had been carrying on extensive speculations, [. . .] from which it [the trade] was just recovering when a revolt in our American colonies reduced it to a very low situation, in so much, that, in the year 1781, the balance, for the first time during the century, was against us; but, with the war [against Revolutionary France and its allies], that disadvantage disappeared. [. . .]

It is evident from this chart that the trade of this country was almost in its infancy at the beginning of the last century; and [is] now great beyond example. We shall farther on in this work have an opportunity of seeing that public expenditure has increased nearly in the same proportion. It is impossible to behold this rapid progress without concluding that it must come in time to a point which it cannot pass, as nothing is infinite; it is therefore of great importance to trace and find out to what causes we owe our commercial superiority, that we may endeavour to prolong it as much as possible; for, though it may be a question admitting of discussion, whether wealth, and what is commonly called commercial prosperity, is any real advantage to a nation, there can be no question that the loss of it, after having once enjoyed its possession, is a very severe misfortune.[73]

The charts, in sum, are designed both to illustrate historical change and to stimulate reflection on it, such reflection being, in a common Enlightenment view, essential to the prudent conduct of present affairs. In Playfair's own words, "it is not from the present state of things, uncompared with the past, that any conclusion can be drawn."[74] Just as present action needs to be informed by knowledge and understanding of history, so the primary function of historical study, to Playfair as to most Enlightenment writers, is to inform and guide present policy.[75] Playfair's ambition—once again charac-

---

[73]*Commercial and Political Atlas*, 3rd ed., pp. 1–2, in *The Commercial and Political Atlas and Statistical Breviary*, ed. Howard Wainer and Ian Spence. Playfair goes on to discuss the important role of credit in trade: "It may not perhaps be improper here to observe, that the great extent of our trade, though owing in part to the good quality of our manufactures, is still more favoured by the long credit we give to foreigners; for those who keep store-houses, shops, or magazines abroad, can fill them with English goods on credit, whereas they must pay almost ready money for commodities manufactured at home, they therefore not only find a facility in procuring British merchandize, but they prefer selling, for ready money, what they can replace upon credit. From this it arises that English goods are in a manner forced upon the consumers, and that those who deal in them, being eager to sell, do it on a moderate profit. It is to a well-managed system of paper credit that we owe the power of doing this, as the real monied capital of the nation is in a great measure absorbed by the public funds." (pp. 6–7)

[74]Ibid., Introduction, pp, xi-xii.

[75]"However much, at first sight, Mr. Burke's opinion [on the difficulty of establishing "permanent causes" and general laws in history; see below] may appear to militate against such an Inquiry, when duly considered it will be found, not only to approve of the end, but to point out the manner in which the inquiry ought to be conducted; namely, by consulting history. If

teristic of the Enlightenment—was to discover, on the basis of empirical research, the regularities and fundamental "laws" of historical development, i.e. the underlying cause and effect relations that he assumed determine the fortunes of states far more effectively than contingent events and accidents, however spectacular these might be. In the Preface to his *Inquiry into the Permanent Causes of the Decline and Fall of Powerful and Wealthy Nations* (1805) he endorses Burke's skepticism with regard to the common belief that states follow the regular, inevitable biological cycle of all living things, that they "have the same periods of infancy, manhood, and decrepitude, that are found in the individuals who compose them." Burke, he says, was right to insist that, whereas "individuals are physical beings, subject to laws universal and invariable," "commonwealths are [. . .] artificial combinations, and, in their proximate efficient cause, the arbitrary productions of the human mind." Whatever laws might govern them, in consequence, cannot be those that govern natural organisms, nor need they have the character of inevitability of the latter. At the same time, Playfair emphasizes that "far from denying the operation of such causes"—i.e. causes reflecting the laws governing the destinies of "commonwealths"—Burke took care "to distinguish things of accident" or "foreign causes" from "permanent causes" claiming only that the permanent causes, "are [. . .] much more obscure, and much more difficult to trace than the foreign causes that tend to depress, and, sometimes, overwhelm society." Burke, in short, "not only admits the existence of permanent causes, but says, clearly, that it is from history they are discoverable, if ever their discovery can be accomplished," although it remains doubtful "whether the history of mankind is yet complete enough, if ever it can be so, to furnish grounds for a sure theory on the internal causes, which necessarily affect the fortune of a state."[76] This, in Playfair's judgment, "is going as far as we could wish"—the more so as Burke does acknowledge the overwhelming influence of such "permanent causes." It is these "permanent causes, that is to say, causes that are constantly acting, and produce permanent effects" that are the primary object of Playfair's own historical investigations.[77] The relation of the permanent causes, or "laws," of historical change to the accidental ones is explained in the manner of Montesquieu in his *Considérations*: "When the Romans were in their vigour, their city was besieged by the Gauls, and saved by an animal of proverbial stupidity; but this could not have happened when Attila was under the

---

it is allowed that any practical advantage is to be derived from the history of the past, it can only be, in so far as it is applicable to the present and the future; and, if there is none, it is melancholy to reflect on the volumes that have been written without farther utility than to gratify idle curiosity." (*An Inquiry into the Permanent Causes of the Decline and Fall of Powerful and Wealthy Nations* [London: Greenland and Norris, 1805], Preface, p. x) Playfair also cites, in support of his thesis about the importance of historical study, "the opinion of a writer of great information and first-rate abilities . . . the intimate friend and biographer of Dr. Adam Smith"—i.e. Dugald Stuart, who preceded Playfair's brother John in the chair of mathematics at Edinburgh. (*Inquiry*, p. xiv and note)

[76]*Inquiry*, Preface, pp. v–vi, quoting Burke.

[77]*Inquiry*, Preface, pp. v, vii, viii–ix.

walls, and the energy of the citizens was gone. The taking or saving the city, in the first instance, would have been equally accidental, and the consequences of short duration; but in the latter days, the fall of Rome was owing to PERMANENT [caps. in text] causes, and the effect has been without a remedy."[78]

Playfair's position, however, was not fatalistic. He had the Scottish Enlightener's moderate confidence in the ability of the enlightened human intelligence to intervene in the course of events and to influence it. He was certainly disturbed by the increasing taste for luxury in the England of his time and by the less and less favorable balance of the nation's trade, which he saw as the consequence of that taste, and he viewed earlier examples of "decline and fall" in history with a degree of resignation as well as alarm. The first chart in the *Inquiry* (a foldout "Chart of Universal Commercial History from the Year 1500 before the Christian era to the present Year 1805"), an adaptation of Priestley's biographical chart to the life of states, situates the powerful and wealthy nations along a regular time line from left to right, marked off at the foot of the frame by centuries and major historical events and divided into two main horizontal segments. The oldest states (entitled "Ancient Seats of Wealth and Commerce") are placed in the lower pink-colored segment, where they are arranged in ascending vertical order from Egypt by way of the Assyrian Empire to Greece, followed by Carthage, Rome, Alexandria, and Constantinople. The modern states, placed in the upper blue-colored segment, are likewise arranged in ascending vertical order from Spain, Venice, the Hansa towns, Flanders, and Holland to France, England, and Russia. A special, narrow yellow-colored segment at the very top right corner of the chart is reserved for America, which thus opens the newest era in the history of states. Each state is represented not by a simple line, as each biography is in Priestley's chart, but by a band the width of which varies according as the relative power and wealth of the state changed over time. The pattern of rise and decline of the great states in history is thus immediately visible to the eye, as is the shift of wealth and power to the modern European states and among the latter, in the course of time, from Venice, Flanders, and the Hansa towns to France and England, and at the very top, in its own segment, to the emerging American Republic [figs. XVI*, 96].

Nevertheless, Playfair rejected simple analogies (France and Rome, England and Carthage, for instance) and he did not believe in passive acceptance of anything resembling the so-called "Tytler Cycle" (widely attributed, without any evidence whatsoever, to his contemporary and compatriot Alexander Tytler), according to which all societies go through stages from bondage by way of religious "enthusiasm," courage, and liberty to abundance, selfishness, complacency, and apathy, only to revert at the end of the cycle to dependence and bondage. To the contrary, the reason for studying the "Decline and Fall of Powerful and Wealthy Nations" in the past was pre-

---

[78]"Unless it be ripe for ruin, a nation never falls; and when it does fall, accident has only the appearance of doing what, in reality, was already nearly accomplished." (*Inquiry*, Preface, p. xii)

cisely to discover through empirical investigation what underlying social, economic, and political conditions might have caused their decline[79] and, in light of what had been learned, to devise and adopt policies that might avert or at least delay the decline of states currently at a high point of development—as England was, according to Playfair, in his own day. The third book of his *Inquiry*, he announced in the Preface, "will begin with an application [to the present state of England] of the information obtained" in the previous books—concerning both the "internal causes of decline; that is to say, all those causes which arise from the possession of wealth and power operating on the habits, manners, and minds of the inhabitants; as also on the political arrangements, laws, government and institutions, so far as they are connected with the prosperity or decline of nations" and the "exterior causes of decline, arising from the envy of other nations, their advancement in the same arts to which the nations that are rich owe their wealth, or their excelling them in other arts by which they can be rivalled, reduced or subdued." It will compare the situation of present-day England "with that of nations that were great" and endeavor "to point out a means by which its decline may be prevented."[80]

It hardly needs to be emphasized that Playfair's method of "illustrating" history—as he himself was at pains to point out—was not well suited to traditional historical narratives with their individual actors and events. It supposed instead an impersonal historiography and focused historical questions, the answers to which would be based on the discovery and comparison of quantifiable and thus comparable data. In view of the suitability of Playfair's charts to the proclaimed goals of Enlightenment historiography and the increasing respect of the age for statistical information, it is surprising that his method was not more widely and rapidly adopted than it was, especially in his own country. Several reasons have been proposed for this: Playfair's somewhat shady reputation, a longstanding distrust in scholarly circles of the visual as appealing more to the senses and the imagination than to reason and as prone to be deceptive, and a few instances where Playfair could indeed be faulted for having used charts in an arguably deceptive manner—a practice that, incidentally, has by no means disappeared.[81] The cost of

---

[79]"One of the most solid foundations on which an inquirer can proceed in matters of political economy, as connected with the fate of nations, seems to be by an appeal to history, a view of the effects that have been produced, and an investigation of the causes that have operated in producing them." (*Inquiry*, Bk. 1, ch. 1., p. 1).

[80]*Inquiry*, Book I, ch. 1, p. 6.

[81]See *The Commercial and Political Atlas and Statistical Breviary*, ed. Howard Wainer and Ian Spence, Introduction, p. 31; also H.G. Funkhauser, "Historical development of the graphical representation of statistical data," *Osiris*, 3 (1937): 269–404, at pp. 292–93. Wainer and Spence (Introduction, p. 10) quote Robert Hooke—whose own *Micrographia* (1665) contained images of items ranging from cloth and urine crystals to plants and animals, as seen under a microscope, but who "used illustrations [. . .] with misgivings": "Pictures of things which only serve for ornament or Pleasure, or the Explication of such things as can better be describ'd by words is rather noxious than useful, and serves to divert and disturb the Mind, and sways it with a kind of Partiality or Respect." For modern examples of misleading graphics, see Edward R. Tufte, *The Visual Display of Quantitative Information* (Cheshire, CT: Graphics Press, 1983), Ch. 2 "Graphical Integrity," pp. 53–58.

preparing and printing charts is also likely to have played a role. The indifference of historians in particular can perhaps be attributed to the fact that the new historiography envisaged by some Enlightenment writers was preached more than it was practiced and was, in any case, soon overtaken by Romanticism. As it came to be placed or to place itself in the service of the nineteenth-century nation-state, history continued to be mostly political history. It thus remained far more concerned with individual acts and actors that lend themselves readily to traditional narrative treatment than with the impersonal developments that Voltaire, Eden, and Playfair thought should be the subject matter of a modern historiography.[82] To be sure, the nation was no longer represented by its dynastic rulers; it became itself the hero of a narrative. "La France," in Michelet's memorable formula, "est une personne."[83] Where visual images did accompany the text of historical works (chiefly, as we shall see, works intended for popular consumption or for the classroom), they were traditional representations of individuals and events, such as battle scenes, death scenes, and dramatic encounters of prominent actors on the historical stage rather than statistical charts.

---

[82]Nevertheless, even a work that could well have benefitted from Playfair's charts—*An Estimate of the Comparative Strength of Great Britain during the Present and four Preceding Reigns; and of the losses of trade from every war since the Revolution* by fellow-Scot, sometime lawyer in Baltimore, and Loyalist in the American War of Independence, George Chalmers (London: John Stockdale, 1786; several subsequent editions)—made no use of them, though the 1794 edition contained a large foldout table listing the number of ships leaving British ports, the value of exports, the balance of trade, and the revenue to the Exchequer from customs for the years 1663, 1688, 1697 and every subsequent year down to 1791.

[83]"Préface de 1869," *Histoire de France*, Bk. III, in *Oeuvres complètes*, ed. Paul Viallaneix, 21 vols. (Paris: Flammarion, 1971-1987), vol. 4, p. 11.

V

Statistics and Graphics in the Nineteenth Century

Playfair's charts did come into their own over the course of the nineteenth century,[84] but not among the best known and most widely read historians. There are no graphics in Ranke, Macaulay, Guizot, or Michelet. The condition for their increasing adoption in the nineteenth century was the Enlightenment's legacy, albeit simplified and flattened, of confidence in the power of positive science to illuminate and resolve or mitigate social problems, such as crime, poverty, and disease; the appetite for statistics, including historical statistics, that accompanied that belief; and the eagerness of the increasingly powerful middle class to demonstrate, by historical comparisons, the "progress"—but also, among the more reform-minded, the shortcomings—of the nineteenth century in relation to the ages that had preceded it. "Enthusiasm for statistical studies increased by leaps and bounds between 1830 and 1850," according to one scholar.[85] A Statistical Society was founded in Manchester in 1833, the Statistical Society of London (as of 1887 the Royal Statistical Society) was formed in 1834; statistical societies were also established in Glasgow (1836), Bristol (1836), Liverpool (1837), Leeds (1838), and Belfast (1838). The Glasgow society declared its aim to be "to collect, arrange, and publish facts illustrative of the condition and prospects, with a view to the improvement, of mankind."[86] Pioneer soci-

---

[84]E.J. Marey notes that while "l'invention de Playfair a mis longtemps à se répandre, [. . .] dès le commencement du siècle, Frissard, ingénieur des ponts et chaussées, construisit en France des tableaux figuratifs du cours des assignats, puis du cours de la rente. Un tableau en trois grandes feuilles fut dressé pour la période qui s'étend de 1789 à 1807. En dehors de ces applications, on peut citer aussi des courbes statistiques relativement à la production métallurgique pendant une longue série d'années. La Hongrie a adopté cette forme de publication pour la statistique de toutes ses productions. L'Amérique adopte également le système des courbes pour ses statistiques annuelles." (*La Méthode graphique dans les sciences expérimentales et principalement en physiologie et en médecine* [Paris: G. Masson, 1885], pp. 31–33).

[85]Funkhauser, "Historical development," *Osiris*, 3 (1937), p. 310.

[86]As reported in "Provincial Statistical Societies in the United Kingdom," *Journal of the Statistical Society of London*, vol. 1, no. 1 (1838), pp. 48–51, 114–18, on p. 116. In France the Société de Statistique Universelle, the predecessor of the Société de Statistique de Paris (1860), was founded in 1829, and, as in Great Britain, societies also took root in the provinces: in the

ologists making extensive use of statistics, such as Adolphe Quetelet in Belgium (*Sur l'homme et le développement de ses facultés: Essai de physique sociale*, 1835; *Du Système social et des lois qui le régissent*, 1848; *Sur la statistique morale et les principes qui doivent en former la base*, 1848) and André-Michel Guerry in France (*Essai sur la statistique morale de la France*, 1833), enjoyed an international reputation. While tables continued to be the predominant method of communicating statistical information for some time,[87] there was also a growing appreciation of the advantages of visual techniques. Guerry, for instance, included a number of coded maps and a large bar chart in his *Essai* [fig. 97] and Florence Nightingale used a pie chart—her "Coxcomb" as she described it herself—in her 1858 report on *Matters Affecting the Health, Efficiency and Hospital Administration of the British Army* in the Crimean War[88] [fig. 98]. Not coincidentally, the pioneering reformer of nursing care was also the first female member of the Royal Statistical Society, as well as a member of the American Statistical Association. In the 1850s through 1870s frequent international congresses of statisticians were held, at which graphics were displayed and uniform international standards called for. Reporting to the Société de Statistique de Paris on the extensive displays of all types of graphic work at the Exposition Universelle in Paris in 1878, the French statistician Emile Cheysson noted the growing use of graphics everywhere and pointed, in terms that Playfair would surely have endorsed, to their enormous advantage over numerical tables.

> Though born only yesterday, graphics are every day expanding their range of application. There is hardly a single branch of human activity now that does not make use of them. Not surprisingly, for they respond perfectly to a double demand of our age: we are in a hurry, but we require precision. We need information, but we need to get it both quickly and precisely. Graphics satisfy these two conditions perfectly. They enable us

---

departments of Deux-Sèvres (1835), Drôme (1837), Cher (1837), and Isère (1838). The American Statistical Association was founded in Boston in 1839. In Germany, statistical societies were established in Saxony (1831), Lübeck (1841), Stettin (1846), Berlin (1847), Breslau (1847) and Hamburg (1853). (Walter F. Willcox, "Note on the Chronology of Statistical Societies," *Journal of the American Statistical Association*, 29 [1934]: 418–20).

[87] A cursory inspection of the *Journal of the Statistical Society of London* turned up no graphics until the Presidential address of Rawson W. Rawson in November 1885, "International Statistics, illustrated by vital statistics of Europe and some of the United States of America" (vol. 48, no. 4). Rawson used graphics to present data on births, deaths, and marriages in England and Wales 1838–1884, and in Europe 1865–1883, as well as on population growth in all countries of Europe and some of the states of the United States over the same period. Four years later, however, Charles Booth's pathbreaking *Labour and Life of the People* in two massive volumes and a substantial appendix volume (London and Edinburgh: Williams and Norgate. 1889-1891), the contributors to which had first presented their findings to the Royal Statistical Society in May 1887 and May 1888, contained innumerable tables and several sumptuously produced color-coded maps of London in a special folder, but only one statistical graph. In the early volumes (1–4, 1860–63) of the *Journal de la Société de Statistique de Paris*, there are likewise many tables, but no graphs.

[88] See http://dd.dynamicdiagrams.com/2008/01/nightingales-rose/

not only to embrace in a single glance entire series of phenomena, but to discern relationships or anomalies, to discover causes, and to discern laws. They successfully substitute for those mountains of numbers under which truth gets buried and whose secrets can be prized out of them only by the most vigorous and aggressive minds. Graphics are thus perfectly suited to the age of steam and electricity. One could say that they give wings to statistics. Not only do they have the advantage of speaking to the senses and to the mind and of presenting vividly before our eyes facts and regularities that it would be very hard to discern in long numerical tables, they overcome obstacles, such as the differences of language and of systems of weights and measures, that stand in the way of the rapid communication of scientific work. These obstacles do not exist for graphics. A diagram is not German, English, or Italian; everyone immediately grasps relationships of size, position, and color. We can well say that graphics have become the true universal language allowing scholars and scientists from every country to freely exchange ideas and the results of research.[89]

The year 1878 also saw the publication of the now-classic work by the pioneer French photographer and physiologist Etienne-Jules Marey, *La méthode graphique dans les sciences expérimentales et principalement en physiologie et en médicine*, the early chapters of which treat "L'expression graphique des grandeurs et de leurs relations"[90] [fig. 99]. Shortly afterwards, in the Jubilee issue (June 1885) of the *Journal of the Statistical Society of London*, the French geographer, demographer, and historian Emile Levasseur published a long article in French, at the invitation of the Society, on the value of graphics to statisticians, the different types of graphics available, and the uses for which each type was most suitable.

Marey paid handsome tribute to Playfair's "invention" in the early chapters of his book, reproducing and explicating a couple of the Scotsman's charts. In addition, he reproduced Playfair's main arguments in favor of charts: "Anything the mind can conceive and measure with exactness can be expressed graphically in a clear and precise manner: numbers, spatial extension, temporal duration, and forces can all be expressed in the most concise and striking way through the use of graphic charts. [. . .] The memory retains knowledge of this kind of image with ease; whenever we call it to mind we see all the relationships represented in it, whereas numbers can only convey these relationships dimly and obscurely."

Playfair, Marey recounts approvingly, underlined "the clarity that this kind of representation provides. To demonstrate that charts alone can bring out the meaning of a set of statistics, he tells of mendacious claims that were

---

[89]"Les méthodes de statistique graphique à l'Exposition universelle de 1878", *Journal de la Société de Statistique de Paris*, 19 (1878): 323–33, on pp. 323–24.
[90]Title of chapter 1.

circulated about the commerce of England and that nobody refuted [in a note Marey explains that Playfair was referring to the political pamphlets of 'Junius,' according to whom Britain's trade had been in decline since 1769—L.G.], even though their falsehood was demonstrated by statistical documents that were available to all."[91]

Whether he was familiar with Playfair's work directly or only indirectly through Marey, Levasseur also took up most of Playfair's arguments. "One might say," he declared,

> that graphics are to numerical statistics what, in the theatre, action is to exposition. [. . .] Numbers are an abstraction: when the eye has read them, the intellect grasps their meaning; but to do so, it must carry out a series of mental operations, in the course of which it perceives successively each of the numbers aligned in long columns. In order to understand how these numbers are related to each other, it must make an effort which even the most skilful do not find easy. Charts, in contrast, are sensuous forms, images which not only attract and hold our gaze but allow us to perceive and understand at a glance an entire complex of relationships and which make an impression on the mind that is not only more lively but even, in many cases, more profound and more durable than numbers. This is a considerable advantage and it is the main *raison d'être* of graphics.

Like Playfair, Levasseur insists that graphics make no claim to superiority over numbers and tables.

> They are not the prime mover. It must never be forgotten that the lead role belongs to numerical statistics. Anyone drawing up a statistic counts and accumulates units, classifies them, arranges them in groups which he then compares and from which he constructs averages; in short, he acts on the numbers; he enumerates and calculates. That is where everyone has to begin. [. . .] Graphics come into play only after the statistic has been established by means of numbers; they are only a mode of expression, and therefore a subordinate form in statistics.

[91]"Tout ce que l'esprit peut concevoir et mesurer avec exactitude s'exprime graphiquement d'une manière claire et précise: des nombres, des longueurs, des durées, des forces, trouvent dans l'emploi des figures graphiques leur expression la plus concise et la plus saisissante. [. . .]

"La mémoire conserve aisément le savoir d'un tableau de ce genre; quand nous en évoquons le souvenir, nous voyons apparaître tous les rapports qui y sont représentés et que des chiffres n'exprimaient que d'une manière obscure. [. . .]

"L'auteur insiste sur la clarté que donne ce genre de représentation, et, pour montrer que les courbes seules font apparaître clairement la signification d'une statistique, il rapporte que des assertions mensongères sur le commerce de l'Angleterre ont pu circuler sans démenti, bien que leur fausseté fût démontrée par des documents statistiques qui étaient entre toutes les mains." (E.J. Marey, *La méthode graphique dans les sciences expérimentales et principalement en physiologie et en médecine* [2nd ed. Paris: G. Masson, 1885], pp. 1, 3, 13)

FIGURE I* *Chroniques de France* (between 1332 and 1350), "Huns sacking Orleans and Agnan's prayer." London, British Library, Ms. Royal 16 G VI, fol. 7 verso. By kind permission of the British Library. © British Library Board.

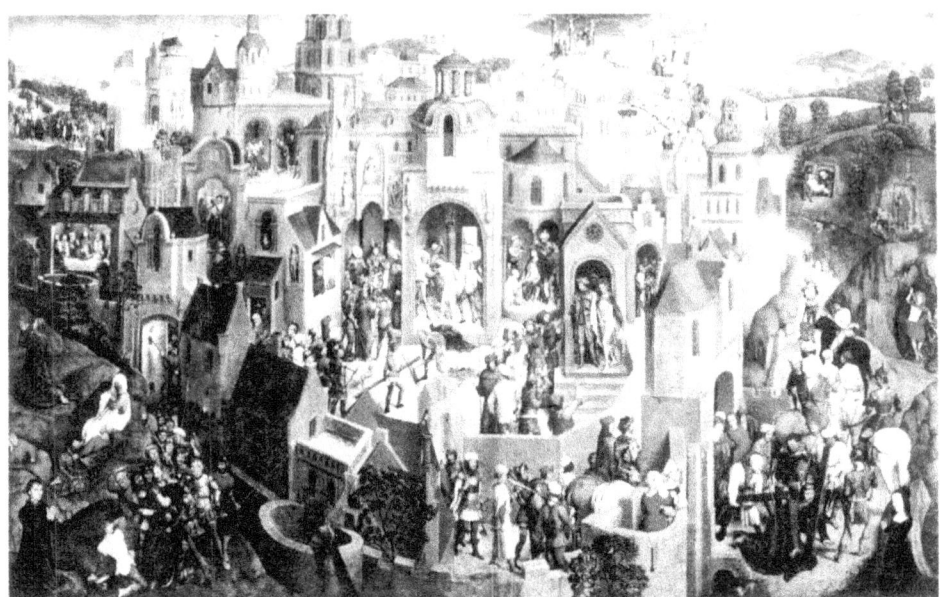

FIGURE II* Hans Memling, "Scenes from the Passion of Christ" (1471). Turin, Galleria Sabauda. Wikimedia Commons.

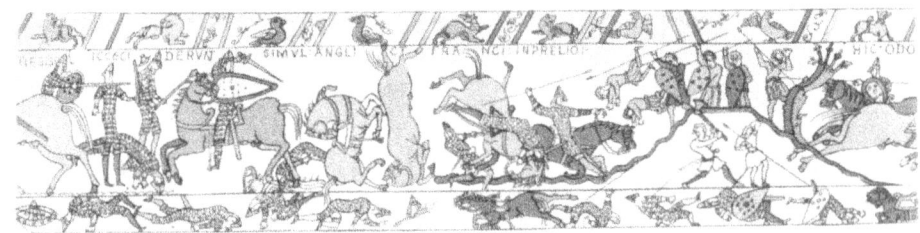

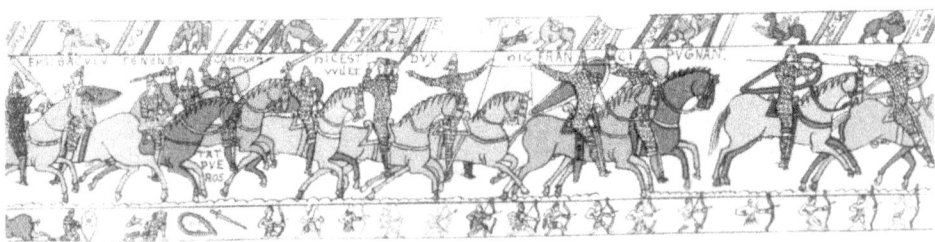

FIGURE IV* Scenes from the Bayeux Tapestry, from John Collingwood Bruce, *The Bayeux Tapestry Elucidated* (London: John Russell Smith, 1856), Plate XV. Princeton University Library.

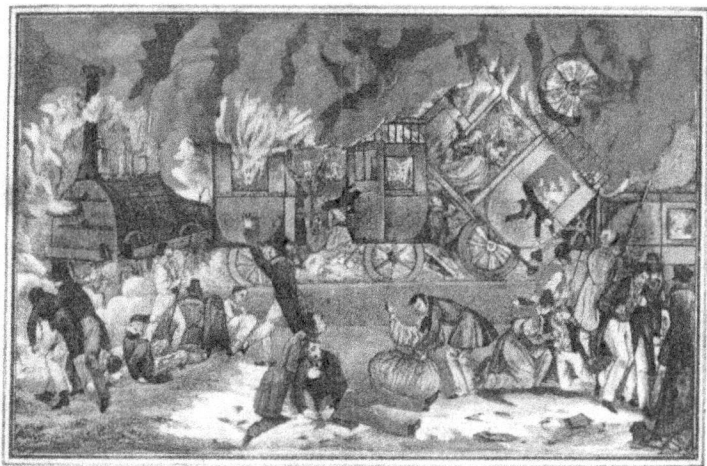

Das große Unglück auf der Eisenbahn zwischen Paris und Versaille

Mehr als hundert Menschen wurden auf einst Jahre auf der Eisenbahn in den verschlossenen Wagen jämmerlich verbrannt. Die Unglücklichen die verschiedenen wollten sich eine Rettungsgeschichte machen, und unternahmen die Reise, doch wie von Berlin nach Potsdam als nicht allein die Gewalt des Dampf, sondern viele persönliche Sachen und das Steuer mit sich gerissene Feuer der Wagen zu Tausenden dennoch verbrannte

FIGURE VII* Neuruppiner *Bilderbogen* (published by Gustav Kühn, 1842). "Terrible accident on the Paris-Versailles railway." http://hu.wikipedia.org/wiki/F%C3%A1jl:Neuruppiner_Bilderbogen_1493.jpg

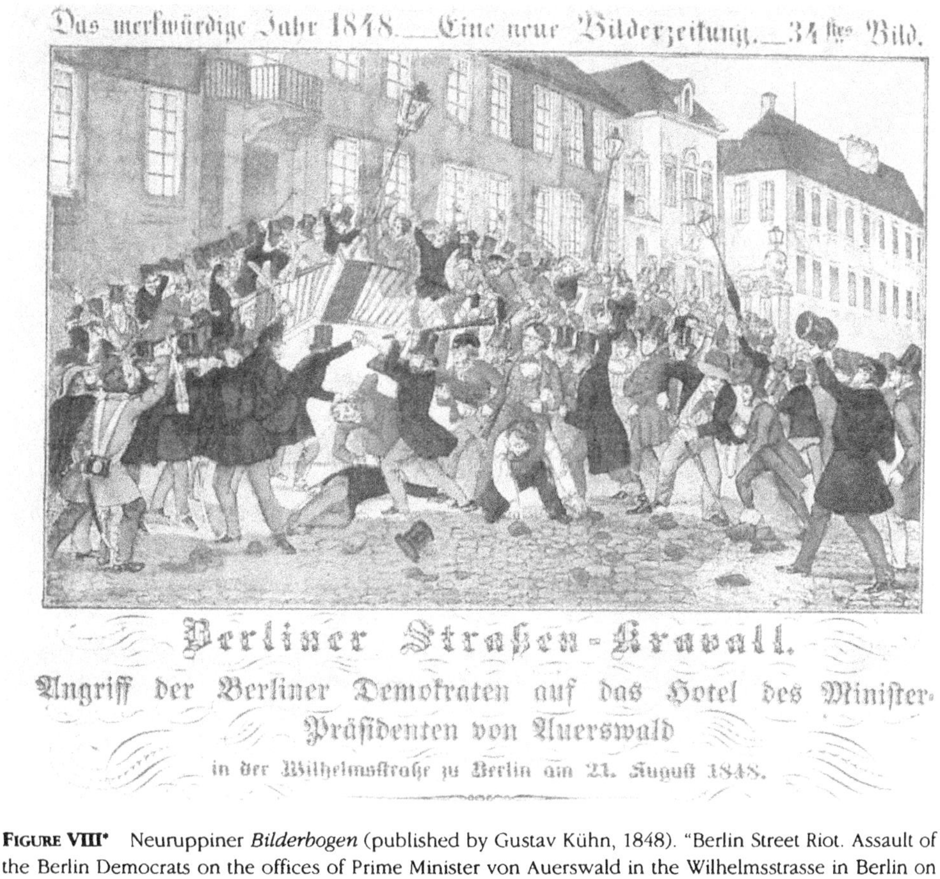

FIGURE VIII* Neuruppiner *Bilderbogen* (published by Gustav Kühn, 1848). "Berlin Street Riot. Assault of the Berlin Democrats on the offices of Prime Minister von Auerswald in the Wilhelmsstrasse in Berlin on August 21, 1848." Wikimedia Commons. http://de.wiktionary.org/wiki/Datei:Auerswald2.jpg

Kampf um Dünkirchen

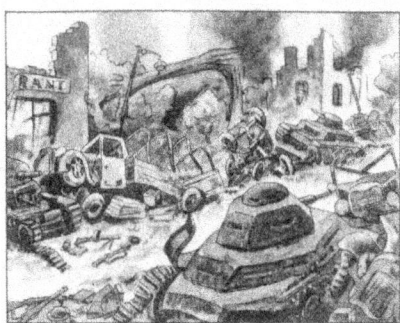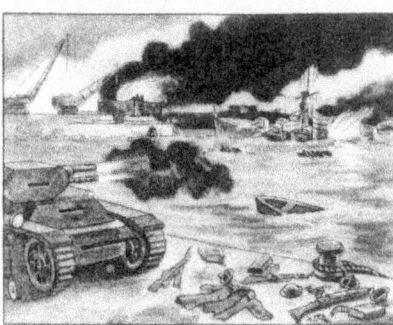

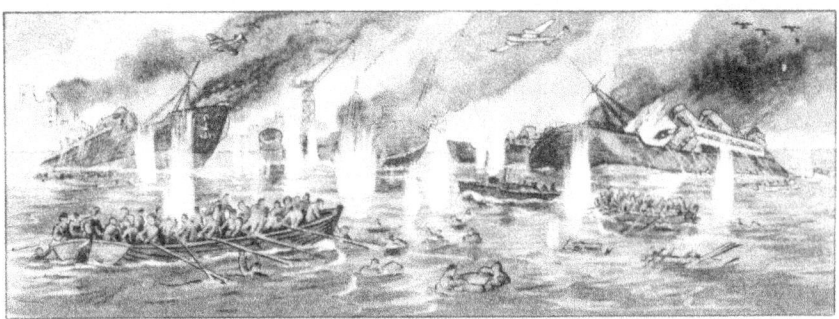

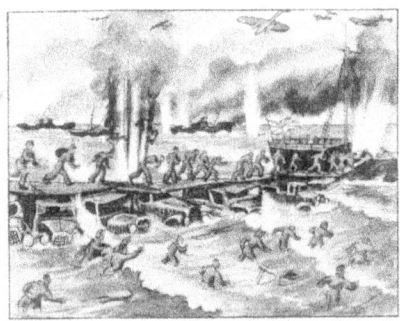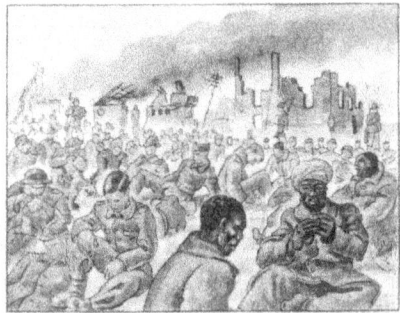

FIGURE IX* Neuruppiner *Bilderbogen* (1940). "Battle of Dunkirk." *Bilderbogen vom Kriege* (Neuruppin: Druck und Verlag Gustav Kühn, n.d. [1941 or 1942]). Cotsen Children's Library. Department of Rare Books and Special Collections. Princeton University Library. Photo: John Blazejewski.

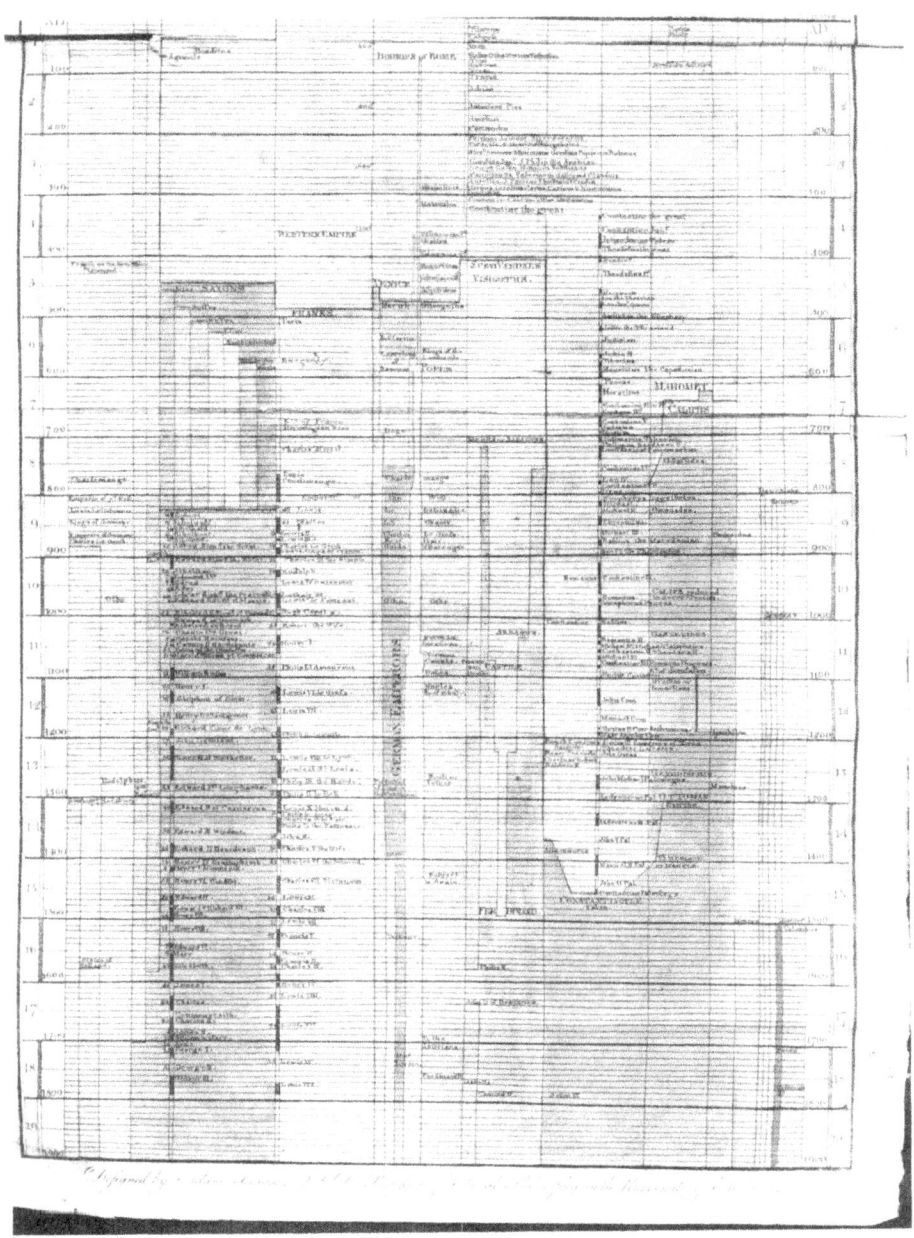

FIGURE XI Time chart (detail) by Adam Ferguson for his article "History," in *Encyclopaedia Britannica*, 3rd ed., Edinburgh: A Bell and C. Macfarquhar, 1797, 18 vols., vol. 8. Princeton University Library.

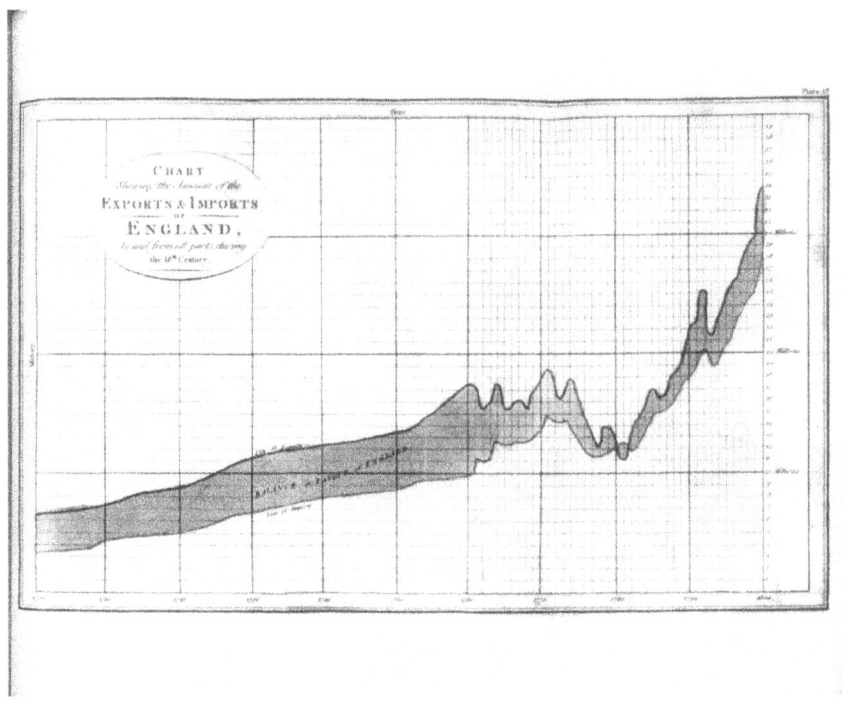

FIGURE XII* William Playfair, *The Commercial and Political Atlas, Representing, by Means of stained Copper-Plate Charts, the Progress of the Commerce, Revenues, Expenditures and Debts of England during the Whole of the Eighteenth Century,* 3rd ed. (London: J. Wallis, 1801 [1st ed. London: J. Debrett, 1786]), chart 1, between p. x and p. 1. Orlando F. Weber Collection of Economic History. Rare Books Division. Department of Rare Books and Special Collections. Princeton University Library.

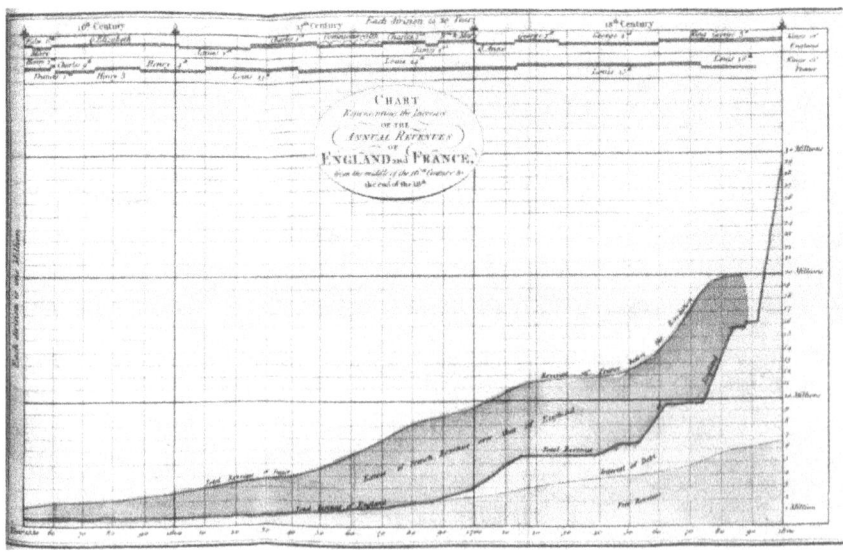

FIGURE XIII* William Playfair, *An Inquiry into the Permanent Causes of the Decline and Fall of Powerful and Wealthy Nations, designed to shew how the Prosperity of the British Empire may be prolonged* (London: W. Marchant printer. Printed for Greenland and Norris, 1805), fold-out chart 4, facing p. 214. Orlando F. Weber Collection of Economic History. Rare Books Division. Department of Rare Books and Special Collections. Princeton University Library. Also in *The Commercial and Political Atlas,* (London: J. Wallis, 1801), chart 19.

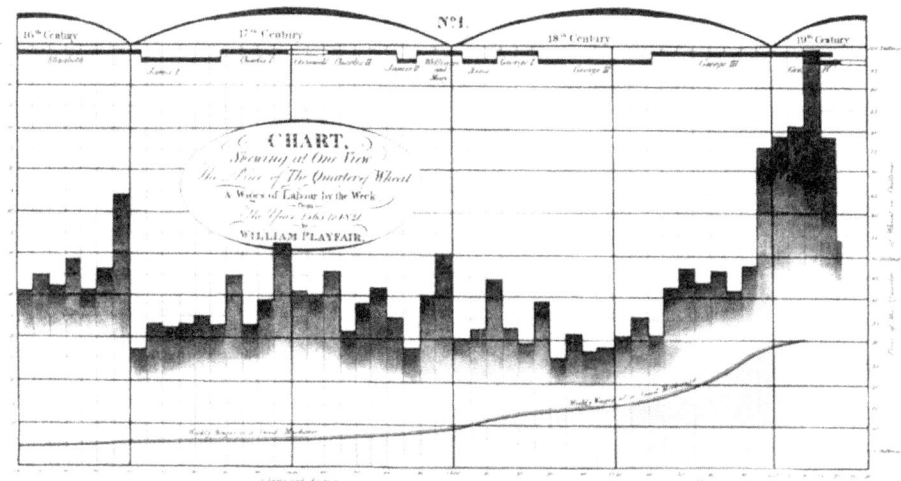

FIGURE XIV* William Playfair, *Letter on our Agricultural Distresses, their Causes and Remedies, accompanied with Tables and Copper-Plate Charts, shewing and comparing the Prices of Wheat, Bread, and Labour from 1565 to 1821. Addressed to the Lords and Commons.* (London: William Sams, 1821), fold-out chart 1. Orlando F. Weber Collection of Economic History. Rare Books Division. Department of Rare Books and Special Collections. Princeton University Library.

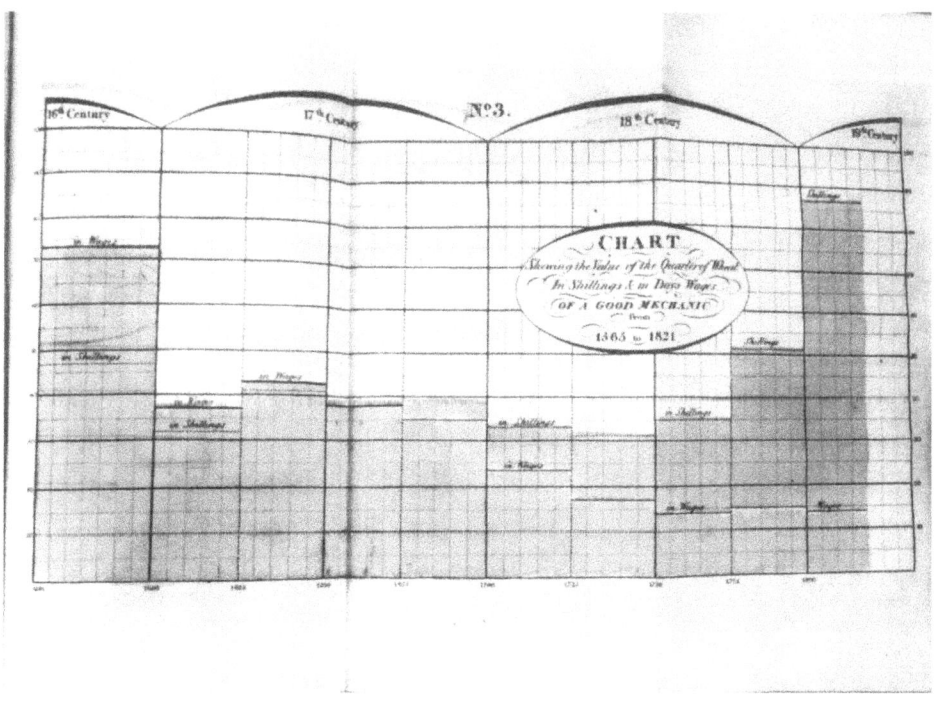

FIGURE XV* William Playfair, *Letter on our Agricultural Distresses, their Causes and Remedies, accompanied with Tables and Copper-Plate Charts, shewing and comparing the Prices of Wheat, Bread, and Labour from 1565 to 1821. Addressed to the Lords and Commons.* (London: William Sams, 1821), fold-out chart 3. Orlando F. Weber Collection of Economic History. Rare Books Division. Department of Rare Books and Special Collections. Princeton University Library.

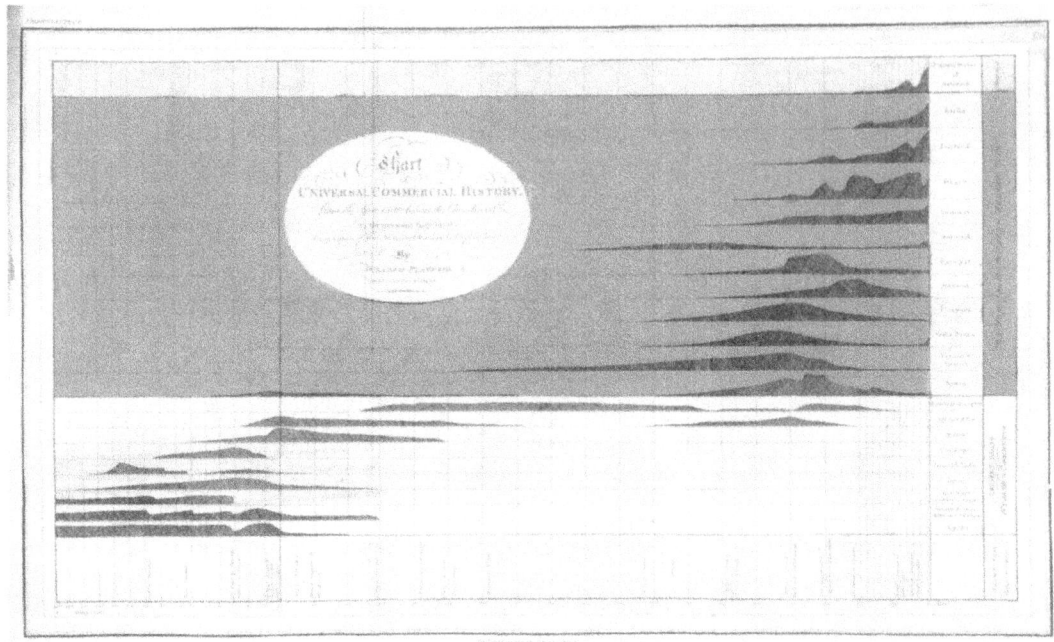

FIGURE XVI* William Playfair, *An Inquiry into the Permanent Causes of the Decline and Fall of Powerful and Wealthy Nations, designed to shew how the Prosperity of the British Empire may be prolonged* (London: W. Marchant printer. Printed for Greenland and Norris, 1805). Extra large fold-out chart facing title-page. Orlando F. Weber Collection of Economic History. Rare Books Division. Department of Rare Books and Special Collections. Princeton University Library. Photo: John Blazejewski.

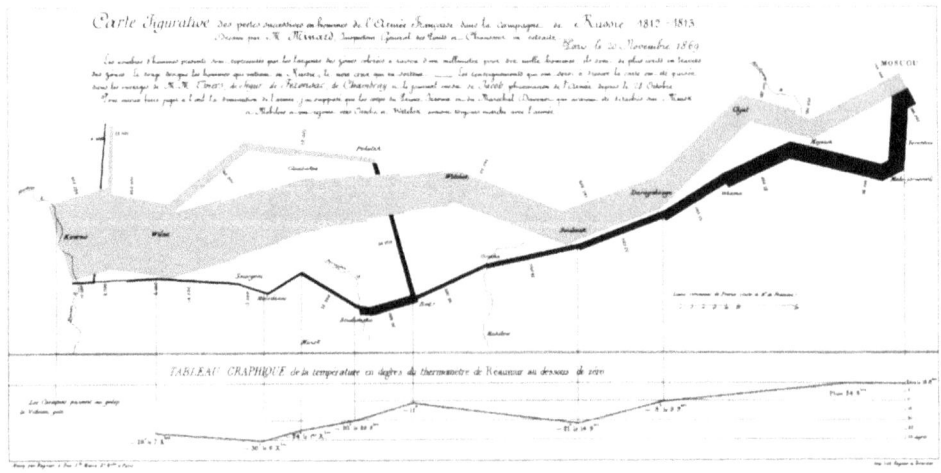

FIGURE XVII Charles Minard, "Carte figurative des pertes successives en hommes de l'Armée Française dans la campagne de Russie 1812-1813" (Paris: Regnier et Dourdet, 1869). http://en.wikipedia.org/wiki/File:Minard.png

> The geometer and the cartographer are given the numbers; it is their job to transform them into graphics that will make their meaning and the relations among them easier to comprehend.[92]

As a teacher, first in lycées in Alençon and Paris and then as Professor of the History of Economic Doctrines (1871–1885) and Professor of Geography, History, and Statistics (1885–1911) at the Collège de France (where lectures are open to the public), Levasseur emphasized that the use of visual aids was "advantageous to statistics above all in popularizing its results" and making them more accessible. A literature for the general reader, in which statistics—including historical statistics—figured prominently, did in fact develop in response to general curiosity about the "progress" of civilization and the achievements of the modern age compared with those that had preceded: the expansion of commerce, communications, literacy, all the "improvements" in which the nineteenth century bourgeoisie took immense pride.[93] The popular books of statistics produced by the prolific Michael G. Mulhall (1836–1900), for instance, provided massive, detailed tables comparing the conditions of the various states of Europe and the territories colonized by Europeans at various times and celebrating the progress of civilization everywhere (especially in the British Isles and the British Empire) and in every conceivable domain—from increasing expectation of life to the growing number of libraries per head of population and of letters carried per person per year. The headings of Part I of *The Progress of the World in Arts, Agriculture, Commerce, Manufactures, Instruction, Railways, and Public Health since the Beginning of the Nineteenth Century* (London: Edward Stanford, 1880) were "Population and Vital Statistics," "Food Supply," "Agriculture and Land Tenure," "Gold and Silver since the 15th Century," "Banks and Paper Money," "Finances and Wealth of Nations," "Commerce and Shipping," "Manufactures, Operatives, Wages," "Minerals: Coal, Iron, Copper, etc.," "Railways, Canals, Tunnels, Bridges, Telegraphs," "Instruction, Schools, Libraries, Press," and "Charities, Pauperism, Crime, Insanity."[94] To bring his message of progress home, Mulhall supplemented

---

[92]Emile Levasseur, "La Statistique graphique," *Journal of the Statistical Society of London. Jubilee Volume* (June 22–24, 1885), pp. 218–50, at pp. 218–19.

[93]E.g. the popular work of G.R. Porter, *The Progress of the Nation In Its Social and Commercial Relations from the Beginning of the Nineteenth Century to the Present Day.* The first edition appeared in London in 1836–38, a second edition in 1843, a third in 1851. As late as 1912, a new edition, brought up to date by the editor of *The Economist*, F.W. Hirst, was put out by Methuen. In William Page's massive 2-volume *Commerce and Industry. A Historical Review of the Economic Conditions of the British Empire from the Peace of Paris in 1815 to the Declaration of War in 1914* (London: Constable, 1919) the entire second volume was devoted to tables of figures outlining revenues and expenditures, shipping, railways, the production of commodities from coal to barley and wool, the imports and exports of various categories of products in all the major parts of the British Empire.

[94]Mulhall, a Dublin-born Catholic, was a committed, patriotic, and liberal Briton. In the texts joining his tables, he leaves no doubt about his opposition to every kind of prejudice—religious, nationalist, and racial. The Chronology at the end of *The Progress of the World*, entitled

his tables with a large number of graphics—bar charts, flow charts, pie charts, and pictograms (in which the relative size of a representational icon, rather than an abstract figure like a bar or a circle, communicates quantity, so that the size of a ship icon, for instance, might convey the size of a merchant fleet) [figs. 100-108].

Though his work was often historical—according to W. W. Rostow, he provided "the most complete statistical portrait of the evolution of international trade after 1720"[95]—Mulhall was not a historian by profession. He was a journalist and a statistician. Nineteenth-century historians, increasingly professionalized and largely focused on the political history on which the identity of the nation-state was founded—hence on narratives involving individual actors and events—were not, in general, drawn either to statistics or to their representation in graphics.[96] It is in no way surprising that one of the most ingenious uses of a diagram to illustrate history, indeed to narrate it, was the work not of a historian but of an engineer. Charles-Joseph Minard's celebrated chart of Napoleon's Russian campaign of 1812, created in 1869—"probably the best statistical graphic ever drawn" in the opinion of Edward Tufte, a pioneer in the modern study of graphics—depicts the fortunes of Napoleon's Grande Armée in the course of its advance to and retreat from Moscow [figs. XVII*, 109]. Beginning on the left at a point representing the Polish-Russian border near the Niemen River, a thick, colored band shows the size of the French army—422,000 men—as it set out to invade Russia in June 1812. As the eye moves from left to right, the width of the band indicates the changing strength of the army (1 millimeter, we are told, represented 10,000 men) in the course of its advance into Russia, with specific numerical figures written in at various points. By the time it reaches Moscow, shown at the extreme right of the chart, the band has narrowed

---

"Record of Progress," is characteristic in its omission of all reference to domestic and international politics and wars and its emphasis on technology and culture. It begins with the year 1801, for which the caption reads "First railway Bill passed," and ends with the caption for the year 1880: "Dr. Siemens' electric railway proposed at Berlin." Similar "events" mark the years in between, e.g. 1812—not Napoleon's disastrous Russian campaign, but "London first city lighted by gas"; 1814—"Times newspaper printed by steam"; 1820—"Ruthven's lithographic press invented at Edinburgh"; 1834 –"Parliament votes £21,000,000 to redeem 770,000 West Indian slaves"; 1855—"Bessemer's system of making steel"; 1857—"Emancipation of Jews in Great Britain"; 1861—"Emancipation of 44,000,000 serfs in Russia"; 1863—"Electric light first used at Havre lighthouse." See likewise Mulhall's *Dictionary of Statistics* (London: George Routledge and Sons, 1886), in which the topics are arranged alphabetically, with "Diamonds," "Diet," "Digestion," and "Disease" following immediately after "Debts of Nations"; his *Balance-Sheet of the World for Ten Years 1870-1880* (London: Edward Stanford, 1881)—almost identical to *The Progress of the World*; and his *Industries and Wealth of Nations* (London, New York, Bombay: Longmans, Green, 1896). Mulhall's work was still being cited in 1965; see David Landes, "Technological Change and Development 1750-1914," *Cambridge Economic History of Europe*, vol. VI, pt. 1 (Cambridge: Cambridge University Press), p. 557, n. 2.

[95]W.W. Rostow, *How it all Began: Origins of the Modern Economy* (London: Methuen, 1975), p. 115.

[96]On resistance of nineteenth-century British historians to the keen interest of the Scottish Enlightenment in statistics and economic history, see D.C. Coleman, *History and the Economic Past* (Oxford: Clarendon Press, 1987), ch. 3.

considerably and numbers inscribed next to it at various critical points indicate that battles, the difficulty of the terrain, and severe weather conditions have taken a huge toll and that the army has already been reduced to 100,000 men. The path of the retreat is represented by a lower-placed, solid black band, starting this time at the right and moving left, and also varying in width and marked at various points with numerical figures. This black band is linked to temperature figures indicated at the bottom of the chart—in recognition of the role played by the extreme cold which caused many of the wounded and hungry to freeze to death. Relevant geographical features, such as rivers, are also marked; thus the disastrous loss of 22,000 lives at the crossing of the Berezina on the retreat is made clearly visible. At the extreme left of the chart (i.e. the Polish border), the solid black band has become a thin line. The number marked on it is 10,000. Minard's chart also shows the movement of auxiliary troops protecting the rear and flank of the advancing army. "Minard's graphic," in Tufte's words, "tells a rich coherent story with its multivariant data, far more enlightening than just a single number bounding over time. *Six* variables are plotted: the size of the army, its location on a two-dimensional surface, [latitude and longitude], direction of the army's movement, and temperature on various dates during the retreat from Moscow."[97]

There were a few special areas of history in which statistics did play a major role, but these were not cultivated by authors generally thought of as historians and even here tables were long preferred to graphics. Among political economists, for example, the Enlightenment's call for a "useful" history that could help resolve the problems of the present retained much of its persuasiveness. The economists' interest in understanding the workings of hidden, impersonal, but—they were convinced—powerfully determining economic forces in history inevitably led them to adopt a statistical approach to the study of the past. This was most noticeable in two areas: the history of prices and the history of trade relations. Volumes 2, 3, 6, and 7 of the monumental 7-volume *History of Agriculture and Prices in England from the Year after the Oxford Parliament (1259) to the Commencement of the Continental War (1793)* (Oxford, 1866–1902) of James E. Thorold Rogers, Professor of Political Economy at Oxford and at King's College, London, and an extremely independent-minded former M.P., consisted of nothing but tables of data; even in the other volumes, the author's interpretative and explanatory text had to share space with tables. In his preface, Rogers "anticipate[d] that the facts and comments contained in these volumes will attract but few readers," for "the form of such a work is necessarily repulsive, and the dry details of business transacted many centuries ago will have but little charm for the general public." Echoing Eden's remarks of seventy years earlier,

---

[97]Edward R. Tufte, *The Visual Display of Quantitative Information* (Cheshire, CT: Graphics Press, 1983), p. 40; also id., *Beautiful Evidence* (Cheshire, CT: Graphics Press, 2006), pp. 126–29. Surprisingly, the one element not clearly indicated in Minard's chart is the temporal one. The reader assumes a uniform representation of time on the chart, but no time markers are given, except for the dates accompanying a few of the temperature indications

however, Rogers insists that "there is nevertheless contained in these relics no small portion of the bygone life of the English people, perhaps even some materials which may aid in constructing a philosophy of history [by which he meant not a metaphysics, but those "laws" that Burke and Playfair hoped to discover—L.G.] by giving depth and solidity to the political events which have been narrated by our annalists."[98] The deep movements that shape events and that escape the attention of "our annalists" with their focus on the glittering surface of history—that "surface agitation of waves thrown up by the powerful movement of tides" in the words used later by the French historians of the *Annales* school[99]—are an essential field of research for the historian, according to Rogers. "The economic interpretation of history [. . .], I venture on asserting, is as important an aid towards the comprehension of the past as the study of legal antiquities, of diplomatic intrigues, or of military campaigns."[100]

As one might expect, Rogers also retains the Enlightenment emphasis on the present "utility" of history, in contrast to what he perceives as the Romantic use of history as an escape from the present: "The study of the past history of the English people, as distinguished from the annals of its government, has a deeper and more permanent significance than the gratification of that refined curiosity which avoids the present by lingering in the past." It causes us to reflect, says Rogers, on the character of the nation's present social life "and especially of its economic features," on the fact that a "great part of the nation has no share in [. . .] the benefits of our prosperity [. . .]. Nor is the bearing of such facts as will be found recorded in these volumes without its meaning on those maxims of political economy, the adoption of which is destined at no remote period to become the chief function of wise government." For "some of the problems of political economy [. . .], I venture on stating, can be discerned and determined with greater ease from the facts which I am able to bring before my reader, fragmentary as they sometimes are, than they could be out of the wider information of our own time. Thus, for instance, the laws which govern prices will, I think, be seen more clearly in these medieval records than they could be in a modern Price Current."[101] Though Rogers was critical of predecessors such as Fleetwood and Eden—his reliance on vast and systematic archival research rather than gleanings from the occasional published volumes of antiquarians dis-

---

[98] Rogers provided such a history of "the bygone life of the English people" in his *Six Centuries of Work and Wages: The History of English Labour* (London: Swan Sonnenschein, 1884)—a readable text, richly informed by Rogers' research, but without the vast statistical apparatus of the massive seven-volume *History of Agriculture and Prices*. There were further editions in 1903, 1909, and 1912, and the work was republished, as it well deserves to be, by Allen and Unwin in London in 1949. A Canadian reprint appeared in 2001.

[99] Fernand Braudel, *Ecrits sur l'histoire* (Paris: Flammarion, 1969), p. 12.

[100] J.T.R. Rogers, *History of Agriculture and Prices in England from the Year after the Oxford Parliament (1259) to the Commencement of the Continental War (1793)* (Oxford: Clarendon Press, 1866–1902), vol. 1, Preface, p. vi.

[101] Ibid., pp. viii–x.

tinguishes his work radically from theirs—his remarks on the "utility" of history are very much in the spirit of Eden.[102]

Rogers was not the only scholar interested in the history of prices. His *History* had been preceded by the *History of Prices and of the State of the Circulation* (6 vols., London, 1838–1857) of the businessman, economist, and Free Trade advocate Thomas Tooke, and he had counterparts in Germany and France: Georg Wiebe's *Zur Geschichte der Preisrevolution des XVI. und XVII. Jahrhunderts* (Leipzig, 1895) had over 60 pages of tables, while Georges d'Avenel's 7-volume *Histoire économique de la propriété, des salaires, des denrées et de tous les prix en général depuis l'an 1200 jusqu'en l'an 1800* (Paris, 1894–1926) offered not only an engagingly written text— volumes 1 and 2, d'Avenel claimed, were nothing less than a history of the rich and propertied, while vol. 3 presented "l'histoire des pauvres"—but thousands of pages of supporting statistical tables.

The history of trade, closely related to that of prices, was another specialized area in which statistics played a major role. Virtually the entire second volume of Georg Schanz's two-volume *Englische Handelspolitik gegen Ende des Mittelalters* (Leipzig: Dunckel und Humblot, 1881), a detailed study of English commercial policy and trade with all the major countries of Europe during the reigns of Henry VII and Henry VIII, consisted of statistical tables [fig. 110]. These list the volume and value of imports and exports of a wide range of goods at various English ports (London, Southampton, Hull, Ipswich, Newcastle-on-Tyne and many others). The two volumes of the classic, still often-quoted study of trade through the Øresund (the narrow sound linking the Baltic and the North Sea) prepared by Nina Ellinger Bang—*Tabeller over skipsfart og varetransport gennem Ørsund 1497–1660* (Copenhagen: Nordisk Forlag, 1906, 1924)—are likewise, as the title indicates, a massive work of statistical compilation and organization. The remarkable Nina Bang, one of the first women to get a degree at a Danish University and later, in 1924, the world's first woman cabinet minister, had indeed studied history and had taught it at the high school level, but she was not a professional historian. She spent most of her life in politics, as a Marxist social democrat.

---

[102]The "usefulness" of the historical study of wages and prices and its relevance to contemporary social and economic policies are vividly confirmed by the fact that Sir William Beveridge, who, among other things, updated Rogers' work in his *Prices and Wages in England from the Twelfth to the Nineteenth Centuries* (London: Longmans, Green, 1939), was also the author of the celebrated Beveridge Report of 1942, which laid the groundwork for the post-War British welfare state and in particular for the National Health Service.

VI

Statistics and Graphics Enter Professional Historiography

Finally, by the early decades of the twentieth century, under the pressure of a massively destructive and destabilizing war and a devastating global economic depression, the field of professional history began to open up to questions that could not be answered by using the critical and investigative methods of political history. The walls of the profession had already been breached in places, no doubt in response to the growing prestige of science and of new disciplines like sociology and economics that seemed better-equipped to study the forces active in modern mass societies. Though the predominant mode of historical writing in the last years of the nineteenth century and the early years of the twentieth was still narrative, still based on unique historical facts and events, and still focused on the nation-state and its individual representatives as the principal actors,[103] it was already being challenged in the name of a "scientific" approach to the past, which was identified at first with sociology, the study of society rather than of the state, of patterns of behavior rather than particular actions, and of human groups rather than individuals. "Tenter la constitution de l'histoire science est un ouvrage qui s'impose à notre temps," declared Paul Lacombe (1834–1919) in a work of 1894 in which the *Inspecteur général des bibliothèques et des archives* recommended the reconciliation and fusion of history and sociology: "The point is not simply to make use of vast quantities of material that have so far contributed almost nothing to our understanding. There is an urgent need to lighten an immense burden weighing on our intellect. The only way to reduce the weight of recorded phenomena is by establishing links among them, and such links can only take the form of a scientific generalization."[104] A few years later in 1903, sociology threw down the gauntlet

---

[103] The definition of history in the 1694 *Dictionnaire de l'Académie*—"the narration of actions and things worthy of memory"—was still retained in the 1935 edition.

[104] "Il s'agit non seulement d'utiliser les matériaux en nombre immense, dont jusqu'ici le profit est presque nul; mais il y a surtout urgence à alléger l'esprit d'un faix qui devient écrasant.

dramatically in what had become something like an institutional competition, when Emile Durkheim announced that "History cannot be a science except by rising above the individual, at which point it ceases to be history and becomes a branch of sociology."[105] In that same year, the economist François Simiand entered the fray with a now-celebrated article, "Méthode historique et science sociale," which he published in Henri Berr's recently founded, innovative *Revue de synthèse*. Simiand denounced the three "idols" of the traditional historian: the "political idol"—i.e., the preoccupation with the state and with political history; the "individual idol"—the inveterate habit of conceiving history in terms of the individuals who allegedly "made" it; and the "chronological idol"—the focus on the search for and study of origins.

Amid the seemingly intractable economic difficulties of the post–World War I period—the reparations issue, currency fluctuations, and finally the Wall Street crash of 1929 and the Great Depression that followed—it is not surprising that a growing number of younger scholars in the ranks of the historians themselves were no longer satisfied with the practices of their elders, above all their emphasis on politics and individual actions, and their blind fidelity to a traditional form of literary narrative (at a time when in literature itself traditional forms of narrative were being seriously challenged by a new generation of writers).[106] They rediscovered earlier work (already referred to here) on the history of prices and they turned for guidance and

---

On ne diminue le poids des phénomènes recueillis qu'en les liant, et ce lien ne peut être qu'une généralisation scientifique." (P. Lacombe, *De l'Histoire considérée comme science* [Paris: Hachette, 1894], Preface, p. xi)

[105]*L'Année sociologique*, 6 (1903): 124–25, quoted in François Dosse, *New History in France. The Triumph of the Annales*, trans. Peter V. Conroy II (Urbana and Chicago: University of Illinois Press, 1994; orig. Fr. *L'Histoire en miettes*, 1987), p. 11.

[106]In the brief account of the history of his book in the preface to the first edition of *La Méditerranée* (Paris: Colin, 1949) Fernand Braudel gives a sense of the change that was taking place. In its earliest form, he relates, when he began work on it in 1923, it was to be a classic historical study of the Mediterranean policies of the Spanish king Philip II. "Mes maîtres d'alors l'approuvaient fort. Ils la voyaient se rangeant dans les cadres de cette histoire diplomatique, assez indifférente aux conquêtes de la géographie, peu soucieuse [. . .] de l'économie et des problèmes sociaux; assez méprisante à l'égard des faits de civilisation, des religions, et aussi des lettres et des arts, ces grands témoins de toute histoire valable, et qui, calfeutrée dans son parti pris, s'interdisait tout regard au delà des bureaux de chancellerie, sur la vraie vie, féconde et drue. Expliquer la politique du Roi Prudent, cela signifiait avant tout établir des responsabilités, dans l'élaboration de cette poltique, du souverain et de ses conseillers, au gré des circonstances changeantes; déterminer les grands rôles et les rôles mineurs [. . .]" (pp. xi–xii) [My teachers at the time strongly approved of it. They saw it fitting into the pattern of a diplomatic history indifferent to the achievements of geography, little concerned with economics and social problems, and rather disdainful of facts relating to culture, religion, and literature and the arts, those great witnesses to any worthwhile history. Shuttered up in its chosen area, this kind of history did not allow itself to look beyond diplomatic papers to the dense richness of real life. An interpretation of the policies of the Prudent King entailed above all establishing the role played by the king and his counselors in elaborating them, through changing circumstances; determining who played major roles and who minor ones [. . .] See also Lucien Febvre's energetic four-page critique of Louis Halphen's *Introduction à l'histoire* (1946), "Sur une forme d'histoire qui n'est pas la nôtre," in *Annales: Économies, Sociétés, Civilisations*, 3 (Jan.–Mar. 1948): 21–24.

inspiration to those economists who were looking into history as part of their search for a better theoretical understanding of the impersonal workings of economic forces. Little by little, quantitative statistical methods were adopted by historians; initially by economic and demographic historians.

Along with statistics came—more slowly and hesitantly—the use of graphics. The early students of the history of prices and of trade—Rogers, Wiebe, and Bang—had made no use of graphics. As late as 1919, William Page, editor of the well-known *Victoria History of the Counties of England*, included only one graphic in the large second volume—consisting of nothing but statistical tables of all aspects of economic activity—of his *Commerce and Industry: A Historical Review of the Economic Conditions of the British Empire from the Peace of Paris in 1815 to the Declaration of War in 1914* (London: Constable, 1919; rprt. New York, 1968; Elibron Classics series, 2005) [fig. 111]. Even Sir William Beveridge's monumental 1939 update of Rogers, with hundreds of pages of tables, contained no charts.[107] Perhaps these writers retained something of the distrust of the visual as seductive and appealing to the senses and the imagination rather than to reason and the mind that had long been common among scholars—even though flowcharts and bar-charts, unlike representational images, are quite abstract and require to be "read" not simply viewed.[108] Emile Levasseur, who had made the case for graphics to the Statistical Society of London in 1885, stands out as something of a pioneer in the academic world. In his three-volume *La Population française: histoire de la population avant 1789 et démographie de la France comparée à celle des autres nations* (1889–92) and again in *La France et ses colonies (géographie et statistique),* also in three volumes (1890–93), the Professor of Geography, History, and Statistics at the Collège de France "enriched his text," as he put it, "with a great number of numerical tables," to which were added, "when it seemed useful to do so"—which proved to be very often—"des cartes de statistiques et des diagrammes par courbes qui font apercevoir d'un coup d'oeil, les variations d'un même groupe de faits"[109] [figs. XVII, 112-120]. Levasseur's interest in graphics had

---

[107]On the relatively late entry of graphics into the *Journal of the Statistical Society,* see note 87 above. Arthur L. Bowley's *Wages in the United Kingdom in the Nineteenth Century* (Cambridge: Cambridge University Press, 1900), which did include a few graphics, appears to have been exceptional at the time of its publication. Bowley made considerably more abundant use of charts two decades later in his *Prices and Wages in the United Kingdom 1914-1920* (Oxford: Clarendon Press, 1921).

[108]According to one scholar, it was generally thought, in the early modern period, that "men 'read' the most abstract of maps, while women merely looked at painted landscapes." (Eileen Reeves, "Reading Maps," *Word and Image,* 9 [1993]: 51-65). If maps were on a par with texts as proper objects of study by rational (male) minds, it is hard to see why statistical graphics would have been regarded disdainfully.

[109]"Statistical graphs and flow charts that make the fluctuations of a single set of facts immediately visible to the eye." (*La France et ses colonies (géographie et statistique)* [Paris: Delagrave, 1890–93], vol. 1, p. ix) Levasseur also included tables and graphics in the many sections he contributed to a profusely illustrated account of the geography, demography, culture, and history of Brazil, of which he was also the editor: *Le Brésil* (Paris: H. Lamirault, 1889). The graphics in his work cover an enormous range of data: comparative demographics

CHAPITRE III. — LA POPULATION ET LA RICHESSE.   79

Les versements aux Caisses d'épargne ont plus que décuplé. Il est vrai qu'une grande part de cet accroissement est due à la loi qui, en 1881, a porté de 1,000 à 2,000 fr. le montant du livret individuel et autorisé le versement intégral de cette somme en une fois. Néanmoins la part réelle des petites épargnes réalisées

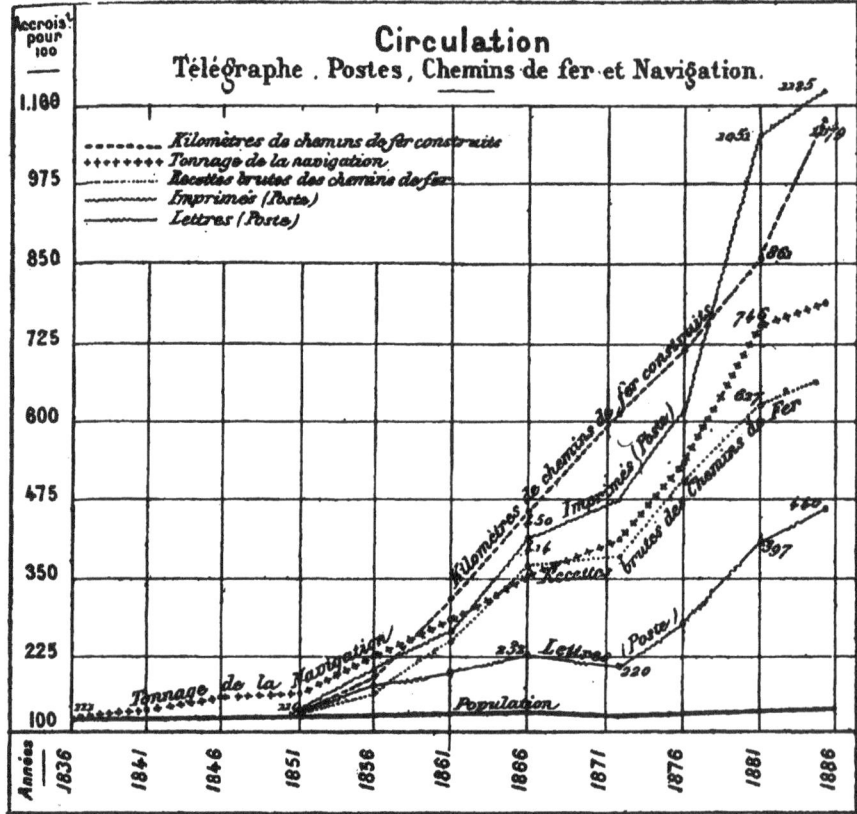

Fig. 156. — Circulation : Télégraphes, Postes, Chemins de fer, Navigation (1836-1885).

par des ouvriers, des domestiques, des employés, des artisans ou des bourgeois s'est considérablement accrue.

Quelque extension qu'aient pris — hors des limites rationnelles de l'institution — les dépôts aux Caisses d'épargne, ils ne représentent que la moindre partie des épargnes qui, chaque année,

FIGURE XVII Emile Levasseur, *La Population française. Histoire de la population avant 1789 et démographie de la France comparée à celle des autres nations au XIXème siècle*, 3 vols. (Paris: Arthur Rousseau, 1889-1892), vol. 3, p. 79. Princeton University Library.

(birth rates, population growth, distribution, and density, patterns of emigration), commerce and finance (trade patterns, revenues from taxes on various articles of consumption, exchange rates), and general wellbeing as measured by changing rates of school attendance, the use of modern means of communication, such as postage, telegraph, railways, and steamships, the quantities of textiles consumed, etc.

been spurred in all likelihood by a keen consciousness of his responsiblities as an educator. In his 1885 address to the London Statistical Society, he claimed that he had been making use of graphics for seventeen years in his teaching at the Collège de France, the Conservatoire des Arts et Métiers, and the Ecole Libre des Sciences Politiques and had also been using them "to introduce some notions of economic geography into secondary and even primary school teaching."[110] His enthusiasm for tables, maps, flow, and bar charts appears to have had little immediate resonance among his colleagues in the field of professional history, however. In fact, graphics seem to have found a place in history textbooks for schools and colleges before they were admitted to works of original historical research[111] [figs. 121-123]. Mention should be made, however, of the handsome graphics produced in 1906 for a demographic atlas of Italy (*Atlante di demografia e geografia medica d'I-talia in 78 Tavole con note illustrative* [Rome: Istituto Geographica Dott. G. De Agostini]) by Enrico Raseri, head of the Direzione Generale di Statistica del Regno and professor of demography at the University of Rome. Many of Raseri's graphics represented historical change[112] [figs. 124–126].

For their part, the economists to whom the younger generation of historians now looked for inspiration had been quicker to recognize that graphics offered them an invaluable rhetorical and communicative tool—a way of summarizing an argument and presenting it more effectively than through

---

[110]Levasseur had been charged by Victor Duruy, the Minister of Education under Napoleon III and a prolific historian himself, with modernizing the teaching of history and geography in the French school system. His *La France et ses colonies* (1st ed., 1867) was intended for use in state-run *lycées* and *collèges*, and it is likely that the addition of graphics in later editions was decided on with the book's readers in mind.

[111]A textbook of 1915, P.W. Tickner's *A Social and Industrial History of England* (London: Edward Arnold), bears witness to a change in the teaching of history in English, but while it was well illustrated with images from the past (rather than illustrations by modern artists), it contained no statistical graphics. Only a few years later, however, in the United States, Abbot Payson Usher's *The Industrial History of England* (Boston and New York: Houghton Mifflin, 1920), "planned and written with a view to the needs of college classes beginning work in economic history," according to the author himself in his Preface, contained many tables and a fair number of graphics. In England the Oxford University Press published in 1925 *An Economic History of England 1066–1874* by Charlotte M. Waters, a retired headmistress of the County School for Girls in Bromley, Kent. "There are signs nowadays," the author declared in the opening sentence of her Preface, "that teachers are anxious to replace a great deal of the political history now taught, by a study of the life and business of the common people, but they find it difficult to obtain books suitable for their purpose." Some social histories have appeared, she goes on, "but most of them are written for lower and middle school children. On the other hand the standard economic histories are too full for any but adult students. This book aims at something in between." No claim is made for original research. Her book is based, Waters acknowledges, on "various standard histories already written." It is, however, a well-designed, well-written, and comprehensive social and economic history, profusely illustrated with well over 200 images drawn from manuscripts and manuscript illuminations, books, broadsides, cartoons, and other similar sources of the period in question; it also features a number of statistical graphics that convey information about economic conditions and trends. Graphics have continued to figure prominently in textbooks for schools; see below, note 172.

[112]Statistical graphics also figure here and there in the work (last third of the nineteenth century) of the internationally renowned geographer (and noted anarchist) Elisée Reclus.

words and tables alone. The most famous of them is no doubt the great Russian economist Nikolai Kondratieff, who argued for his "long waves" theory in the 1920s with the help of graphics based on English, American, and French statistics dating back, in the case of the first two, to the eighteenth century. But Kondratieff was by no means the first economist to make significant use of graphics: Arthur Bowley at the London School of Economics and Henry Ludwell Moore at Columbia, for instance, had already employed them to advantage a decade earlier [figs. 127–133]. Bowley's *Wages in the United Kingdom in the Nineteenth Century* (Cambridge: Cambridge University Press, 1900), which covered many trades and occupations in different parts of the country over the period from 1791 to 1900, included several graphics along with numerous detailed and elaborate tables.[113] Similarly, in the context of practical politics, the author of a report to a U.S. Senate "Commission of Gold and Silver Inquiry" in 1925 made abundant use of graphics to illustrate historical developments and trends in European currency and finance[114] [fig. 134]. The existence of a market for graphics manuals, such as Willard C. Brinton's *Graphic Methods for Presenting Facts* (New York: The Engineering Management Company, 1914), is a clear sign of the growing popularity of graphics. Brinton gave instructions for making various kinds of statistical charts, recommended the best kinds for particular purposes, and warned against inaccurate or deceptive forms of graphic design [fig. 135].

---

[113]N. D. Kondratieff's writings in Russian appeared in the 1920s. There was a German translation in 1926: "Die langen Wellen der Konjunktur," *Archiv für Sozialwissenschaft und Sozialpolitik*, 56 [1926]: 573–609. This was the basis of a later English translation: N. D. Kondratieff, "The Long Waves in Economic Life," *Review of Economic Statistics*, 17 (1935): 105-15. Kondratieff had appended eleven pages of tables to his 1926 article in German as support for the graphics in the text, but these were dropped from the 1935 English translation. Apparently graphics were now deemed capable of standing on their own. For Moore, see his *Economic Cycles: Their Laws and Causes* (New York: Macmillan, 1914).

[114]John Parke Young, Ph.D., *European Currency and Finance. Commission of Gold and Silver Inquiry United States Senate* (Washington: Government Printing Office, 1925). Printed for the use of the Senate Commission of Gold and Silver Inquiry. Foreign Currency and Exchange Investigation, Series 9, vol. 1. Young, a Princeton Ph.D. in Economics, was subsequently head of the State Department's division of international finance. A longtime advocate of a single world currency, he helped draft the original charters of the IMF and the World Bank. Abundant use of graphics was also made by French Ambassador Extraordinary and Plenipotentiary Henry Berenger in a memorandum on *France and her Capacity to Pay* that he submitted to the U.S. War Debt Funding Commission (dated Washington, March, 1926).

VII

The New History

It was François Simiand's student, Ernest Labrousse, who established statistical graphics as a legitimate and essential part of writing generally recognized as "history." Labrousse's *Esquisse du movement des prix et des revenus en France au XVIIIème siècle* (Paris: Librairie Dalloz, 1933), followed a decade later by his enormously influential *La Crise de l'économie française à la fin de l'ancien régime et au début de la Révolution* (Paris: P.U.F., 1943–1944), set the stage for a new kind of historiography. In the words of François Dosse in his 1987 study of the "new history" in France, "the real revolution in history, which absorbed Simiand's inspiration by adapting it to history, came from Ernest Labrousse." Thanks to his research into prices and revenues, Labrousse "succeeded," according to Dosse, "in integrating the long term, the evolution of structures, and the study of events into a single whole that attempted to explain the French Revolution of 1789." He was very quickly seen as "the initiator of an economic history founded on statistics, quantification, and cycles of long and short time periods."[115] Twenty years earlier Emmanuel Le Roy Ladurie had made a similar claim for Labrousse as the initiator of quantitative history. It was not Lucien Febvre or Marc Bloch, the founders of the influential journal that gave its name to the whole modern *Annales* school of historians, who effected "the passage from 'quality' to 'quantity'" in historiography, he told his American colleagues at the annual meeting of the American Historical Association in Toronto in 1967. "L'impulsion première, vers la poursuite du quantitatif, est venue d'un troisième homme, Ernest Labrousse."[116]

Whereas the representational images found in popular history books at a time when they were excluded from the works of "serious" historians had

---

[115]François Dosse, *New History in France*, pp. 51-52. On the emergence of a new historiography in France, see also the admirably clear and concise, slightly earlier study by Peter Burke, *The French Historical Revolution: The "Annales" School* (Cambridge: Polity Press, 1990).

[116]Emmanuel Le Roy Ladurie,"Du quantitatif en histoire: la VIème section de l'Ecole pratique des Hautes Etudes," in his *Le Territoire de l'historien* (Paris: Gallimard, 1973), p. 26. Le Roy Ladurie made the same point in an article in *Le Monde* (25 January, 1969): "Les spécialistes d'histoire économique, depuis Levasseur, Hauser et Mantoux, ont toujours utilisé les chiffres; la chose allait de soi. Mais c'est vers 1932, avec les grands livres de Simiand et de Labrousse que l'usage systématique de la quantité a pris force de loi chez les historiens." (*Territoire de l'historien*, p. 15).

been intended, as we shall see, to enhance the already considerable appeal of such narrative texts to the reader's imagination by "bringing to life" key episodes, leading characters, and heroic actions, the graphics in Labrousse were intended to clarify and make vivid an historical argument that was addressed to the reader's intellect. The same can be said for Henri Hauser's *Recherches et documents sur l'histoire des prix en France* (Paris: Les Presses modernes, 1936), even though Hauser still relied heavily on tables to demonstrate the movement of prices from the sixteenth century on. In the English-speaking world, the Williams College professor C. F. Remer used a number of graphics in his historical study of *The Foreign Trade of China* (Shanghai: The Commercial Press, 1926) while the pioneering studies of Earl J. Hamilton—*American Treasure and the Price Revolution in Spain 1501–1650* (Cambridge, MA: Harvard University Press, 1934), followed thirteen years later by his *War and Prices in Spain 1651–1800*, with the same publisher—made abundant use of both tables and graphics. In Germany, the first volume of John Moritz Elsas's massive *Umriss einer Geschichte der Preise und Löhne in Deutschland vom ausgehenden Mittelalter bis zum Beginn des neunzehnten Jahrhunderts*, published during the author's exile in Holland (Leiden: Sijthoff, 1936)—publication of the entire work was interrupted by the invasion of Holland and the author's flight to England and the two parts of the second volume appeared only after the war—contained many graphics [figs. 136–138]. Though influenced by ideas about the role of economic forces in history and richly informed by their authors' familiarity with economics (Remer was a professor of economics at Williams, then at the University of Michigan, Hamilton also started his career as a professor of economics), the works of Labrousse, Hauser, and Hamilton were generally seen as products of the history workshop. Through them and works like them, statistical graphics gained admission to academic historiography.[117] By the 1950s and 1960s they had become a fairly common feature of historical writing, especially, to be sure, in the areas of demographic and economic history[118] [figs. XIX, 139–155].

---

[117]While Hamilton occupied a chair of economics for many years, he was elected President of the Economic History Association in the early 1950s and ended his career as Professor of Economic History at the State University of New York. His work quickly became known to and highly regarded by general historians of Spain; see, for instance, John H. Elliott, "The Decline of Spain" (*Past and Present*, 1961, reprinted in Trevor Aston, ed., *Crisis in Europe 1560–1660* [London: Routledge and Kegan Paul, 1965], pp. 167-94). According to Elliott, now Regius Professor of History at Oxford and a leading authority on Spanish history, Hamilton provided the "classic statement of the theme" of the decline of Spain.

[118]Some examples: A.M. Carr-Saunders, *World Population: Past Growth and Present Trends* (Oxford: Clarendon Press, 1936)—with no fewer than 60 graphics; A. Chabert, *Essai sur les mouvements des revenus et de l'activité économique en France de 1798 à 1820* (Paris: Librairie de Médicis, 1949); Michel Mollat, *Le Commerce maritime normand à la fin du Moyen Âge: étude d'histoire économique et sociale* (Paris: Plon, 1952); Phyllis Deane and W.A. Cole, *British Economic Growth 1680–1959* (Cambridge: Cambridge University Press, 1962); E.M. Carus-Wilson (a student of the legendary Eileen Power), *England's Export Trade 1275–1547* (Oxford: Clarendon Press, 1963); Y. Le Moigne, "Population et subsistances à Strasbourg au XVIIIème siècle," in *Contributions à l'Histoire démographique de la Révolution française* (Paris: Commission de recherche et de publication des documents relatifs à la vie

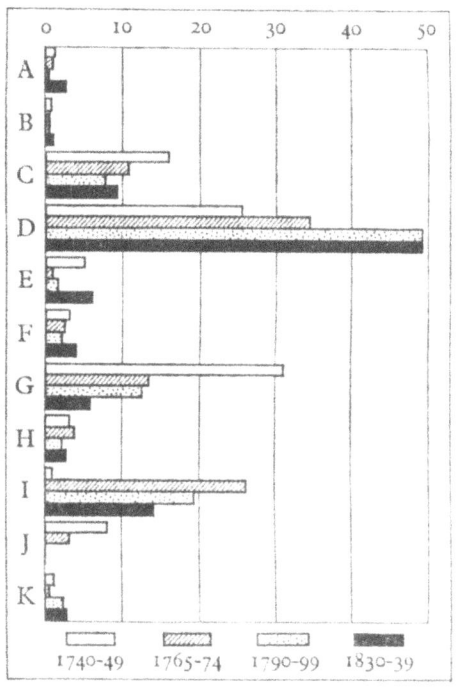

21. ORIGINES SOCIALES DES ÉTUDIANTS A L'UNIVERSITÉ DE GLASGOW AU XVIIIe SIÈCLE
(D'après les chiffres de W. M. Mathew,
« *Glasgow Students, 1740-1839* »,
in Past and Present, *n° 33, 1966.)*

A. Administration. — B. Armée, marine. — C. Église. — D. Industrie et commerce. — E. Loi. — F. Médecine. — G. Nobles et propriétaires fonciers. — H. Enseignants. — I. Petits exploitants. — J. « *Citoyens* ». *— K. Divers.*
L'Écosse vient largement en tête, au XVIIIe, de la diffusion en profondeur de la culture écrite. L'avance de l'alphabétisation se répercute à tous les échelons de l'échelle du savoir que nous avons proposée (v. p. 146). Au niveau le plus élevé, le savoir universitaire. Celui-ci déborde de plus en plus sur des secteurs sociaux modestes qui, nulle part ailleurs en Europe, n'accèdent encore à ce niveau élevé de la connaissance. Le plus étonnant, c'est la part des petits exploitants, l'équivalent de nos laboureurs et haricotiers, plus du quart un moment. Là réside un des secrets du rôle des Écossais dans le développement technologique à l'époque de Watt. Tout aussi significative, la permutation entre noblesse-propriétaires fonciers et industrie-commerce. Voilà la grande ouverture. Industrie-commerce : 50 p. 100. Tout un monde qui ne se contente plus d'être intelligent avec les mains. L'accès de cette couche sociale à l'université va transformer le savoir universitaire.

FIGURE XIX "Social origins of students at Glasgow University in the eighteenth century," in Pierre Chaunu, *La Civilisation de l'Europe des Lumières* (Paris: Arthaud, 1971), *graphique* 21, p. 145. By kind permission of the publisher.

Even as the use of graphics has increased in tandem with the increased role of statistics and quantitative analysis in the work of modern historians, some champions of "quantitative history" have questioned the depth of the shift in emphasis in historical research away from the traditional nineteenth-century narrative of meticulously investigated and documented actions and events. The introduction of the quantitative element into history has been "timide et fragmentaire," Jean Marczewski, a proponent of rigorous quantitative methods, charged in 1964. "The statistics used by economic historians have served essentially to characterize a structure at a given moment, or to illustrate a development over a period of time, or to express the interrelated-

économique de la Révolution, Mémoires et Documents, vol. 14, 1962), pp. 11–44; and two early studies by Michel Vovelle, who would go on to extend the use of quantitative methods and of graphics to aspects of cultural history: "Les taxations populaires de février-mars et novembre-décembre 1792 dans la Beauce et sur ses confins," in *Structures sociales et problèmes économiques* (1787–1798) (Paris: Commission de recherche et de publication des documents relatifs à la vie économique de la Révolution, Mémoires et Documents, vol. 13, 1958), pp. 107–59, and "Chartres et le pays chartrain," in *Contributions à l'Histoire démographique de la Révolution française,* pp. 129–59.

ness of two or more series. Significant as they may be, these applications of statistics entail no fundamental modification of the traditional methods of economic history. They do improve our knowledge of particular sets of relations," but "an economic history that uses statistics and statistical data is not truly 'quantitative' as long as its fundamental gesture, the choice of the data to be considered, is not determined by quantitative methods and as long as the conclusions to which it leads cannot be expressed in entirely quantitative terms."[119] In light of this criticism, Pierre Chaunu, one of the most energetic and productive practitioners of a history based on quantifiable, homogeneous series of data—in 1966 he founded a *Centre de recherches d'histoire quantitative* at the University of Caen—proposed that the term "histoire sérielle" be used for the kind of "quantitative" history judged inadequately quantitative by Marczewski.

Without engaging in a lengthy debate with Marczewski, Chaunu explained that in adopting the term "quantitative," the historians of the 1930s and 1940s had simply "wanted to make clear how far removed the new questions being addressed by history were from the old ones, how far the new history was from a chronicle privileging the history of the State, that is, from a history inseparably associated with the methodical search for and investigation of the individual fact, the anecdote, the unique phenomenon tightly and rigorously located at a particular point in time. They wanted to demonstrate that they were aligning themselves to a certain degree with science, insofar as science supposes repetition, measurement, mathematical models—i.e. quantification." He conceded that the term "quantitative" might best be reserved, as Marczewski demanded, for a "global, circular type of quantification, in the form of a comprehensive account-sheet, all the columns of which had been properly filled in and carefully balanced"—that is to say, for a history in which all particular series would be interrelated through their relation to a total structure—something he saw as a Utopian endpoint, "un voeu, un passage à la limite." To describe what modern French historians since Labrousse had been trying to do in a variety of ways, he proposed therefore that the term "histoire sérielle" be adopted. "Let us then use the term 'serial' for everything else, that is to say for what is essential, for all history's efforts to extend beyond its old borders toward the collective, for everything that tends toward the substitution of the significant for the anecdote, toward complementing the critical analysis of the individual item with a demand for the coherency of series [. . .], for everything that culminates, in short, in the great revolution in the methodology of history." If this terminology is acceptable, then for the last twenty years, Chaunu claims (writing in 1970), "history has been serial, one might go so far as to say that it is no longer anything but serial."[120]

---

[119]Jean Marczewski, "Buts et méthodes de l'histoire quantitative," *Cahiers Vilfredo Pareto*, 3 (1964): 125–64, at p. 126.

[120]"Les historiens de l'économie avaient été tentés de revendiquer pour les enterprises nouvelles de l'histoire, à la hauteur des années 1930, 40, 50, l'apposition quantitative. Ils avaient voulu marquer par là la distance qui sépare la nouvelle problématique des problématiques

In his own magisterial "serial history"—the 9-volume *Séville et l'Atlantique (1504–1650)* (Paris: S.E.V.P.E.N., 1955–56)—as well as in the later *Séville et l'Amérique aux XVIème et XVIIème siècles* (Paris: Flammarion, 1977), Chaunu himself made extensive use of statistical series, and graphics played a vital role in their presentation. Volume 6 of *Séville et l'Atlantique* consists of 1000 pages of tables; the information they contain is then presented in lively graphic form in the flow, bar, and pie charts, often combined ingeniously with maps, that occupy the whole of volume 7 [figs. 156, 157]. Graphics, designed by one of Chaunu's co-authors, are also an essential component of a collaborative volume for which he provided both the numbers and the text, *Les Philippines et le Pacifique des Ibériques: XVIème-XVIIème-XVIIIème siècles. Construction graphique* (Paris: S.E.V.P.E.N., 1966).They are likewise prominent in numerous later scholarly studies of trade patterns as indices of larger historical conditions, a fair number of them no doubt inspired, in part at least, by the work of Chaunu[121] [figs. 158–160]. Of one of those, Louis Dermigny's remarkable *La Chine et l'Occident: Le Commerce à Canton au XVIIIème siècle 1719–1833* (Paris: S.E.V.P.E.N., 1964, 3 vols. plus album), Le Roy Ladurie pointedly observed that "as in the case of Chaunu's *Séville*, this is a book that it would not be unreasonable to begin at the end, by 'reading' the magnificent album of graphics."[122] That album, incidentally, contains both statistical graphics and evocative representational images from the period under investigation [figs. 161, 162].

In establishing his distinction between the extremely abstract "histoire quantitative" demanded by Marczewski and the practice of many modern historians, Chaunu seems to have been eager to guarantee and facilitate the extension of the use of quantifiable data by historians to as many areas of history as possible, including those seemingly most recalcitrant to any kind of quantification.[123] Economic history, he wrote in 1965, is no longer in the

---

anciennes, d'une histoire chronique privilégiée de l'Etat, d'une histoire liée à une recherche méthodique du fait individuel, de l'anecdote, de l'expression unique, étroitement et rigoureusement localisée dans le temps. Ils avaient voulu marquer un certain alignement sur la science qui suppose répétition, mesure, modèle mathématique, donc quantification." (Pierre Chaunu, "L'histoire sérielle. Bilan et perspectives," *Revue historique*, 243 [1970]: 297–314, at pp. 298–99). "Nous retiendrons donc, avec Jean Marczewski le terme de quantitatif pour une quantification globale, circulaire, en forme de comptabilité, dont toutes les colonnes seront remplies et soigneusement balancées. [. . .] Pour tout le reste, c'est-à-dire, pour l'essentiel, pour toutes les tentatives de débordement de l'histoire, en direction du collectif, pour tout ce qui tend à substituer à l'anecdotique le significatif, à doubler la critique isolée par l'exigence de cohérence des séries, [. . .] pour tout ce qui débouche, en un mot, sur la grande révolution de la méthodologie historique, bornons-nous à parler de sériel. L'histoire depuis vingt ans est sérielle, à la limite, même, elle n'est plus que sérielle." (Ibid., pp. 300–01)

[121]E.g. Ramon Ferrer Navarro, *La Exportacion valenciana en el siglo XIV* (Saragossa: Consejo Superior de Investgaciones Cientificas, 1977), in which the final 50 pages (pp. 250–300) consist of full-page graphics of annual exports of different products; Lutgardo Garcia Fuentes, *El Comercio español con America, 1650–1706* (Seville: Publicaciones de la EXCMA deputacion provincial de Sevilla, 1980); Jean-Philippe Priotti, *Bilbao et ses marchands au XVIème siècle: Genèse d'une croissance* (Villeneuve d'Ascq: Presses Universitaires du Septentrion, 2004).

[122]*Territoire de l'historien*, p. 28.

[123]Chaunu's definition of "histoire sérielle"—"Une histoire sérielle, c'est une histoire qui code, qui annexe l'aberrant au significatif, c'est une histoire raccordée au présent, une histoire utile,

van of innovation in historiography for it has already carried out its revolution. The revolution in historical studies has now moved to other areas. Already under way, this revolution consists in "annexing the other sectors of human activity in the past so that the methods of serial investigation can be applied to them too." The latest area to be so annexed, according to Chaunu, is the history of religion: "the history of religion is on its way to becoming a serial history."[124] The work of Michel Vovelle—*Mourir autrefois: Attitudes collectives devant la mort aux XVIIème et XVIIIème siècles* (Paris: Gallimard/Julliard, 1974), *Les Métamorphoses de la Fête en Provence de 1750 à 1820* (Paris: Aubier/Flammarion, 1976), *La Mentalité révolutionnaire* (Paris: Editions sociales, 1985)—as well as Chaunu's own *La Mort à Paris: XVIème, XVIIème et XVIIIème siècles* (Paris: Fayard, 1978) has amply justified Chaunu's confidence that the "serial method" could be applied to questions of "mentalité," to the history of religion, of sociability, even of music, art and literature. The history of literature, for instance, has been enriched by the quantitative studies of the history of the book and of reading by scholars like Henri-Jean Martin [figs. 163–169].[125] An ambitious recent attempt to apply quantitative methods and graphics to literary studies may be a harbinger of things to come, even if it remains so far, to the best of my knowledge, unique and tantalizingly brief. In *Graphs, Maps, Trees: Abstract Models for a Literary History* (2005), Franco Moretti, a leading scholar of comparative literature, argues that the trends and structures revealed by quantitative research and made visible in graphics can throw valuable light on a field that "cannot be understood by stitching together separate bits of knowledge about individual cases." This is because, as he puts it, the field "isn't a *sum* of individual cases: it's a collective system, that should be grasped as such, as a whole—and the graphs that follow are one way to begin doing this."[126] Quantitative analysis, Moretti adds, often opens up questions that traditional literary history had not been able to imagine [figs. XX, 170, 171].

---

pourvoyeuse d'indices, une histoire qui emprunte ses problématiques aux sciences de l'homme du présent en les adaptant aux structures du passé"—would probably have made sense to William Playfair. ("Une histoire religieuse sérielle. A propos du diocèse de La Rochelle [1648–1724] et sur quelques exemples normands," *Revue d'histoire moderne et contemporaine*, 12 [1965]: 5-34, at pp. 5–6) In fact, Chaunu explicitly evokes the conception of history developed by "les maîtres dédaignés du XVIIIème siècle" ("L'histoire sérielle. Bilan et perspectives," *Revue historique*, 243 [1970], p. 302).

[124]"Une histoire religieuse sérielle" (as in note 123 above), pp. 5–6.

[125]*L'Apparition du livre* [with Lucien Febvre] (1958); *Histoire du livre*, 2 vols. (Paris: Bibliothèque Nationale, 1964), *Livre, pouvoirs et société à Paris au XVIIème siècle* (Geneva: Droz, 1969), *Histoire de l'édition française*, 4 vols. (Paris: Promodis, 1983-1986). See also the volume of essays, edited by François Furet, on the production and circulation of books in the Eighteenth Century, *Livre et société dans la France du XVIIIème siècle* (Paris and The Hague: Mouton, 1970) or the more specialized article by Christine Théré, "Economic publishing and authors 1566–1789," in Gilbert Faccarello, ed., *Studies in the History of French Political Economy* (London and New York: Routledge, 1998), pp. 1–56.

[126]Franco Moretti, *Graphs, Maps, Trees: Abstract Models for a Literary History* (London: Verso, 2005), p. 4. My thanks to Professor Peter Baldwin for drawing my attention to this essay.

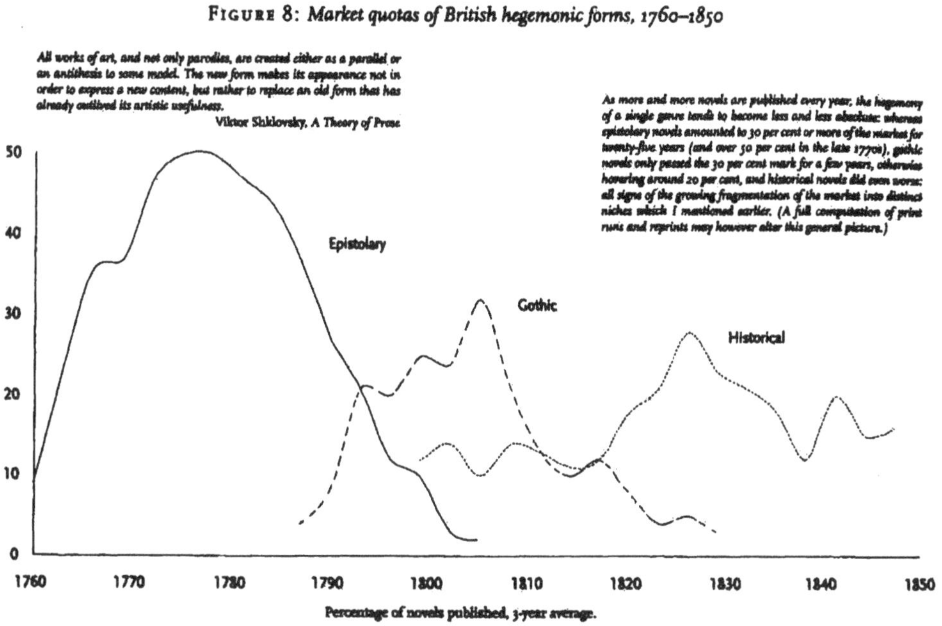

FIGURE 8: *Market quotas of British hegemonic forms, 1760–1850*

All works of art, and not only parodies, are created either as a parallel or an antithesis to some model. The new form makes its appearance not in order to express a new content, but rather to replace an old form that has already outlived its artistic usefulness.

Viktor Shklovsky, A Theory of Prose

As more and more novels are published every year, the hegemony of a single genre tends to become less and less absolute: whereas epistolary novels amounted to 30 per cent or more of the market for twenty-five years (and over 50 per cent in the late 1770s), gothic novels only passed the 30 per cent mark for a few years, otherwise hovering around 20 per cent, and historical novels did even worse: all signs of the growing fragmentation of the market into distinct niches which I mentioned earlier. (A full computation of print runs and reprints may however alter this general picture.)

Epistolary

Gothic

Historical

50
40
30
20
10
0

1760　1770　1780　1790　1800　1810　1820　1830　1840　1850

Percentage of novels published, 3-year average.

FIGURE XX "Market quotas of British hegemonic forms 1760-1850," in Franco Moretti, *Graphs, Maps, Trees: Abstract Models for a Literary History* (London: Verso, 2005), fig. 8, p. 16. By kind permission of the author.

Political history itself has become "serial" as scholars have applied quantitative methods to the study of opinions, attitudes, and voting patterns in the past. As a result, graphics, which figure prominently in all the above-mentioned histories, have now become a fairly common feature of scholarly studies in many fields.

VIII

Representational Images in Historiography: Persistence and Transformation

As has been suggested at various points in this essay, scholarly historians from the sixteenth century until the end of the nineteenth eschewed representational images. There are no illustrations, except for occasional engraved portraits of rulers[127] in Guicciardini or De Thou, in Voltaire, Hume, Robertson, or Gibbon, in Ranke, Droysen, Treitschke, Mignet, Michelet, or the latter's rival Henri Martin; there are none in Macaulay, Hallam, Bury or Grote. One of the reasons for this absence of images may have been the cost of printing them before the invention of inexpensive reproduction technologies in the nineteenth century. It also seems likely, however, that "serious" historians thought of themselves as appealing to the mind rather than the senses, and addressing educated and critical readers capable of responding to words and ideas, without the sensuous stimulation of images. By such historians and such readers the image may well have been deemed not only unnecessary but inappropriate. It belonged to the world of the uneducated, those considered incapable of giving their attention to anything other than an entertaining story, and of the illiterate and of the semi-literate, to whom no text was thought to be accessible that did not also offer the kind of immediate excitement provided by the immensely popular illustrated *Bilderbogen* and

---

[127]As, for example, in the eight-volume 1802 edition of Hume's *History of England* (London: T. Cadell jun. and W. Davies) or a similar eight-volume edition of 1826 (Oxford: Talboys and Wheeler; London: William Pickering), where an engraved image of the appropriate monarch opens the section of the history devoted to that monarch's reign—a pattern familiar from seventeenth-century histories such as Mézeray's *Histoire de France*.

broadsides.[128] As Strabo had observed in the reign of Augustus Caesar, *pictura est quaedam litteratura illitterato*.[129] Serious historians, it would seem, were not immune to a persistent mistrust of visual representation that has long been a feature of Western culture (as well as of some others).[130] A once-common view of painting, never completely eradicated, as a "mechanical" art did not enhance the standing of the representational image.[131] The

---

[128]With the invention of lithography at the end of the eighteenth century, the *Bilderbogen*, until then produced as a woodcut print, took off, especially in Germany and France. The total number of sheets produced by the celebrated printer Gustav Kühn in Neuruppin (Brandenburg) and shipped all over the world had reached 25,000 by 1825 and over a million by 1832. During the war years 1870–71 alone, more than one million were produced. As the sheets were numbered, it is known that in 1825 a single broadsheet was produced in about 500 copies, in 1845 in 1,800 copies and by 1885 in 8,000 copies. The Neuruppiner prints continued to be hand-colored in simple, stark colors until 1890, employing local village labor. On their popularity, see Karl Schottenloher, *Flugblatt und Zeitung* (Berlin: Richard Carl Schmidt, 1922), pp. 434–38, and Elke Hilscher, *Die Bilderbogen im 19. Jahrhundert* (Munich: Verlag Dokumentation, 1977); see also the tribute to them by the great German writer Theodor Fontane in his *Wanderungen durch die Mark Brandenburg*, vol. 1 (Stuttgart and Berlin: J.A. Cotta'sche Buchhandlung Nachfolger, 1906; 1st ed. 1861), pp. 126-28. In France, so-called *images d'Epinal* enjoyed similar popularity and continued to illustrate events up to the First World War. Neuruppiner prints were produced even during World War II to illustrate the heroic exploits of the German army, navy, and air force; see *Bilderbogen vom Kriege* (Neuruppin: Druck und Verlag Gustav Kühn, n.d. [late 1941]) [fig. XII]. In the U.S. Currier and Ives, self-described as "publishers of cheap and popular pictures," turned out 7,500 titles in over one million lithographic, handcolored prints between 1835 and 1907 [fig. 48].

[129]Quoted by Arnold Hauser, *Social History of Art*, (London: Routledge and Kegan Paul, 1951), vol. 1, p. 137. It is generally accepted among writers on the *Bilderbogen* that the latter appealed especially to the less well educated and to those whose reading skills were limited. (See Hilscher, *Die Bilderbogen im 19. Jahrhundert*, pp. 18, 26, citing Adol Spamer, "Bilderbogen" in *Reallexikon der deutschen Kunstgeschichte* [Stuttgart, 1948], vol. 2, p. 549, and Willy Stiewe, *Das Bild als Nachricht* [Berlin: C. Duncker, 1933], p. 12.)

[130]See W.J.T. Mitchell, *Iconology: Image, Text, Ideology* (Chicago and London: University of Chicago Press, 1987) and other writings by this author. Cordula Grewe notes that in religious education "skepticism about the use of images had brought about a widespread exclusion of visual material from teaching in the decades leading up to 1800. Many rationalist educators mistrusted reproductions as teaching tools, fearing that the dominance of the sensual impression gained from printed materials (rather than from *realia*) would diminish the child's already weak capacity for abstraction. [. . .] As late as 1828 the Protestant theologian Curt Grüneisen complained about the weak capacity of 'the people' to detach themselves from the visible and to approach the pure idea (*reine Vorstellung*)." (*Painting the Sacred*, p. 210) This traditional suspicion of images has been remarkably tenacious. Explaining that the passing of the Children and Young Persons (Harmful Publications) Act in the United Kingdom in 1955 (renewed in 1965) was a reaction to the influx of American horror comics after the War, the English literature scholar Stuart Sillars adds: "Later critics may suspect that the origins of this disquiet lay in mistrust of the way in which the intellectually and imaginatively stimulating process of reading had been ousted by the less demanding act of absorbing simple visual images; yet these feelings were strong, and by no means recent. Disapproval of comics [. . .] had been present ever since their first appearance in England at the end of the nineteenth century." (Stuart Sillars, *Visualisation in Popular Fiction 1860-1960* [London and New York: Routledge, 1995], pp. 132-33)

[131]Hence Leonardo da Vinci's defense of painting against the poets' charge that it is a mechanical art: "And if you call painting dumb poetry, the painter may call poetry blind painting. Now which is the worse defect? to be blind or dumb? Though the poet is as free as the painter in the invention of his fictions they are not so satisfactory to men as paintings; for, though poetry is able to describe forms, actions and places in words, the painter deals with

serious historian may well have regarded the work of even the best illustrators as an unworthy distraction from his own.

In contrast, images were by no means disdained in accounts of sensational and dramatic events, whether contemporary, as in single-sheet broadsheets, *Bilderbogen*, and *images d'Epinal*, or past, as in full-scale books. A striking early nineteenth-century example of such a book, consisting of a collection of unrelated historical anecdotes, was published in New Haven, Connecticut in 1826, and was accurately entitled *Museum of History, or Narratives of the most Remarkable and Interesting Events which have taken place in Ancient and Modern Times, containing Authentic Accounts of Wonderful Adventures, Heroic Actions, Perilous Travels and Voyages, Miraculous Escapes, Celebrated Trials and Executions, Noble Examples of Fortitude and Patriotism, Singular and Entertaining Incidents, Eccentric Personages, Stratagems of Warfare, and Feats of Strength and Agility*. This work, its publisher announced proudly on the title-page, was "embellished by 24 engravings" (figs. 172–174).[132] These presumably were intended to enhance the effect of the book, which, according to the preface, was designed to appeal to its readers as "creatures of sentiment and feeling, as well as of intelligence" and, "aside from the many other advantages which [knowledge] affords," to provide "a source of immediate and abundant pleasure." The general histories, produced in ever-growing numbers in the nineteenth century for a new and expanding market of both newly rich "merchants, manufacturers, and other businessmen"—as the *Art Journal* in 1872 described a rising class of collectors of artworks[133]—and modestly literate working people, were also likely to be illustrated, as were similarly market-oriented popularizations, abridgments and, in some cases, de luxe editions of works by well-established historians like Gibbon or Hume.

Nineteenth-century histories dealing with the extraordinary, dramatic events and larger-than-life personalities of the recent, revolutionary past were particularly likely to be illustrated, sometimes even with color engravings. The French Revolution and the exploits of Napoleon—"événements qui tiennent du prodige" ["events that have something miraculous about

---

the actual similitude of the forms, in order to represent them. [. . .] And if the poet gratifies the sense by means of the ear, the painter does so by the eye—the worthier sense; but I will say no more of this but that, if a good painter represents the fury of a battle, and if a poet describes one, and they are both together put before the public, you will see where most of the spectators will stop, to which they will pay the most attention, on which they will bestow most praise, and which will satisfy the best. Undoubtedly painting being by a long way the more intelligible and beautiful, will please most." (From page 16 a-b of a fragment of Leonardo's *Libro di Pittura*, in the Library of Lord Ashburnham. *The Notebooks of Leonardo da Vinci*, edited by Jean Paul Richter, 2 vols. [New York: Dover Publications, 1970], Vol. 1, Sections 653–54.)

[132]The English original by a Rev. Joshua Watts (London: A. Robertson, 1825) had an equally sensational title: *Remarkable Events in the History of Man; or Narratives of the Most Wonderful Adventures, Remarkable Trials, Judicial Murders, Prison Escapes, Heroic Actions and Astonishing Occurrences which have taken place in Ancient and Modern Times.*

[133]Quoted in Mary Cowling, *Victorian Figurative Painting* (London: Andreas Papadakis, 2000), p. 10.

them"] in the words of one author[134]—seem to have been perceived as similar in nature to the wonders and prodigies reported in traditional broadsides, if not as a kind of modern, secular equivalent of the Bible narratives, and they very quickly became the subject of numerous illustrated histories, often by contemporaries and eye-witnesses, such as Jacques de Norvins (1769–1854) or Jacques-Antoine Dulaure (1755–1835). The considerable success of these histories anticipated in fact that of Schnorr's and Doré's illustrated Bibles. As early as 1823, Dulaure's *Esquisses historiques des principaux événemens de la Révolution française; depuis la convocation des États-généraux jusqu'au rétablissment de la maison de Bourbon* (Paris: Baudouin frères, 1823-25) was enlivened by a large number of engraved illustrations by the prolific François-Louis Couché (1782-1849), known as Couché fils [figs. 175-178]. In 1824, *Napoléon et ses contemporains* (Paris: Jules Renouard, 1828) by Auguste de Chambure (1789-1832) contained portraits of all the numerous politicians and, above all, military men whose biographies are traced in it, along with illustrations of scenes exemplifying individual acts of "heroism, clemency, and generosity" [figs. 179, 180]. Even more copiously illustrated, Norvins' four-volume *Histoire de Napoléon* (Paris: Dupont et Cie., 1827-28) was "ornée de portraits, vignettes, cartes et plans" by the seemingly tireless Couché fils. Later editions of Norvins' work, of which there were many, were still more richly illustrated. The seventh edition (Paris: Furne, 1837), for instance, contained numerous engravings after the most celebrated artists contemporary or nearly contemporary with the author and the subject—Antoine-Jean Gros (1771–1835), Horace Vernet (1789–1863), Claude Gautherot (1796–1825), and the immensely productive Denis-Auguste-Marie Raffet (1804–60) [figs. 181–185]. An edition in one volume (Paris: Furne, 1861) was abundantly illustrated by Raffet alone with both full-page engravings and wood engravings in the text. (See below, p. 70 [figs. 203–205].) Specializing in portraits of military men and battle scenes from recent or contemporary history, Raffet by his early twenties had already been a major contributor of illustrations to Adolphe Thiers' ten-volume *Histoire de la Révolution française* (Paris: Lecointe, 1828). Among the many later editions of Thiers' work, the fifth (Paris: Furne, 1836) was enhanced by numerous engravings based on paintings by well-regarded artists such as Ary Scheffer (1795–1858) and Antoine (Tony) Johannot (1803–52) [figs. XXI, 186–189].

Raffet was the principal illustrator of a remarkable book entitled *Musée de la Révolution française. Histoire chronologique de la Révolution française, collection de sujets dessinés par Raffet et gravés sur acier par Frilley, destinée à servir de complément et d'illustration à toutes les Histoires de la Révolution (Thiers, Mignet, Montgaillard, Lacretelle, etc.)* (Paris: Perrotin, 1834; Brussels: Adolphe Wahlen, 1844).[135] This work consisted of detailed—

---

[134]Auguste de Chambure, *Napoléon et ses contemporains* (Paris: Jules Renouard, 1828), Avant-propos, p. v.

[135]Steel engraving, which began to replace copper in the 1820s and 1830s, allowed for smaller and more finely engraved prints.

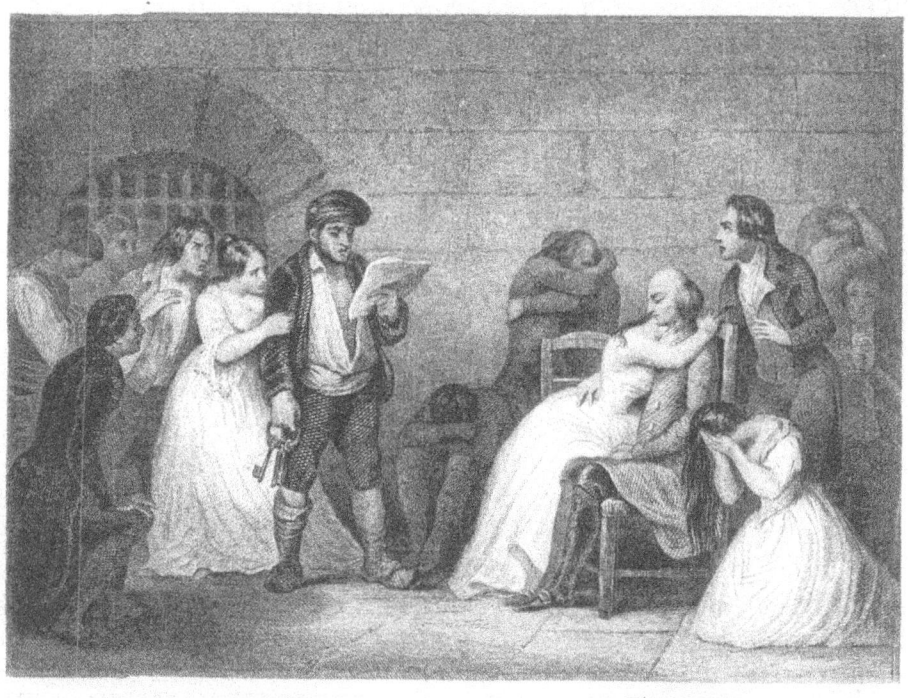

FIGURE XXI   Antoine (Tony) Johannot, "L'Appel des condamnés," in Adolphe Thiers, *Histoire de la Révolution française*, 13th ed., 10 vols. (Paris: Furne, 1845), vol. 6, facing p. 140. Princeton University Library.

at times almost day-by-day—chronologies for every year of the Revolution, each of which was followed by short, two-page narrative accounts of selected events from that year's chronology. Every other page in the volume of 122 numbered pages of text was unnumbered and was an illustration [figs. 190–192]. (It should be noted, however, that the publisher did not claim to have offered the public a history of the Revolution "told in images"; the book was described only as a *"complément"* to any verbal narrative. Despite its wealth of images, in short, the *Musée de la Révolution française* did not challenge the priority of the verbal text as the fundamental vehicle of historical narrative.) In 1845–46, an *Histoire de la Révolution française, du Consulat, de l'Empire, de la Restauration et de la Révolution de juillet* in six volumes by J. Ferrand and J. de Lamarque boasted that it was "ornée de 30 gravures sur acier." These were divided between depictions of important actions and portraits of the chief actors [figs. 193, 194]. Hard on its heels, Louis Vivien de Saint-Martin's six-volume *Histoire de Napoléon, du Consulat et de l'Empire* (Paris: Eugène et Victor Penaud frères, 1848), to which a number of writers contributed, was illustrated with black and white engravings of scenes and episodes and bright color engravings of the uniforms distinguishing the various ranks and units of Napoleon's armies [figs. 195–197]. The poet Lamartine's immensely successful *Histoire des Girondins* (Paris: Furne et Cie., W. Coquebert, 1847), which was immediately translated into English and published in London by Bohn (1847–48) and which went through many editions both in French and in English, at first contained only portraits. However, an "édition illustrée," "publiée par l'auteur" (Paris: Armand Le Chevalier, 1865–66), was provided with copious illustrations by some of the most popular illustrators of the time, including Clément-Auguste Andreux (1829–80) and Alphonse de Neuville (1835-1885), a student of Delacroix. Moreover, the illustrations in this mid-century edition of Lamartine's history were not printed on separate pages, as copper and steel engravings had to be and as had until then been customary, but were produced by the less expensive process of wood engraving, which allowed images to be printed on the same page with the text, as in the rapidly developing popular illustrated magazines [figs. XXII, 198–202]. Many of the images by Raffet illustrating the twentieth edition of Norvins' *Histoire de Napoléon* (Paris: Furne, 1861), condensed now into a single large volume, were printed in the text by the same process of wood engraving [figs. 203–205].[136]

Histories of the Revolution and of Napoleon were clearly in high demand among contemporaries and near-contemporaries of the extraordinary and exciting events they narrated. But as the Revolution had turned entire nations into heroes of history, there was also a growing market for popular national histories, as well as for history textbooks for use in the schools of the nine-teenth-century nation-state, where local boys were to be made into patriotic Frenchmen and Englishmen. These books were almost always illustrated. The first edition, in 1805, of Louis-Pierre Anquetil's *Histoire de France depuis les Gaulois jusqu'à la fin de la monarchie* (Paris: Garnery, an XIII; 14 vols.)— undertaken at Napoleon's suggestion in order to offer the public "une his-toire complète mais succincte, régulièrement distribuée par dates, [. . .] assez étendue pour donner une idée juste des événemens, pas assez volumineuse pour épouvanter le lecteur et le rebuter" (preface, p. iii)—had not been illus-trated; but the numerous subsequent editions, continuously updated by a variety of other historians (Anquetil died in 1806), almost invariably were.[137] Thus the five-volume edition of 1839 (Paris: Furne), which was brought up-to-date by the addition, in the final volume, of an *Histoire de la République française, du Directoire, du Consulat, de l'Empire, de la Restauration et de la Révolution de 1830* by Jacques de Norvins, included engravings of paintings by Gros, Raffet, Scheffer, and Vernet, as well as original engravings by less

---

[136]On wood engraving, see Geoffrey Wakeman, *Victorian Book Illustration: The Technical Revolution* (Newton Abbot: David and Charles, 1973), pp. 17–22, 68–71, and Paul Goldman, *Victorian Illustrated Books 1850-1870: The Heyday of Wood Engraving* (London, British Museum Press, 1994).

[137]Between 1813 and 1866, over thirty-five different Paris publishers put out editions of Anquetil's *Histoire de France*, in various formats from quarto to octodecimo. Many of these editions were also reissued in successive years. The Furne edition, for instance, which first appeared in 1830, was reissued in 1839 (the text consulted by the present writer), 1855–58, and 1865–66. The number of volumes ranged from three to fifteen (though one in-18 edition, put out by Houdaye, filled 33) and a number of different writers were employed by the vari-ous publishers to add the supplemental chapters or volumes required to bring the narrative up to date. While many, probably most, of these editions were already illustrated, the pub-lisher Hocquart brought out a volume entitled *Gravures pour servir à l'Histoire de France d'Anquetil* in 1830.

LIVRE DIXIÈME. 245

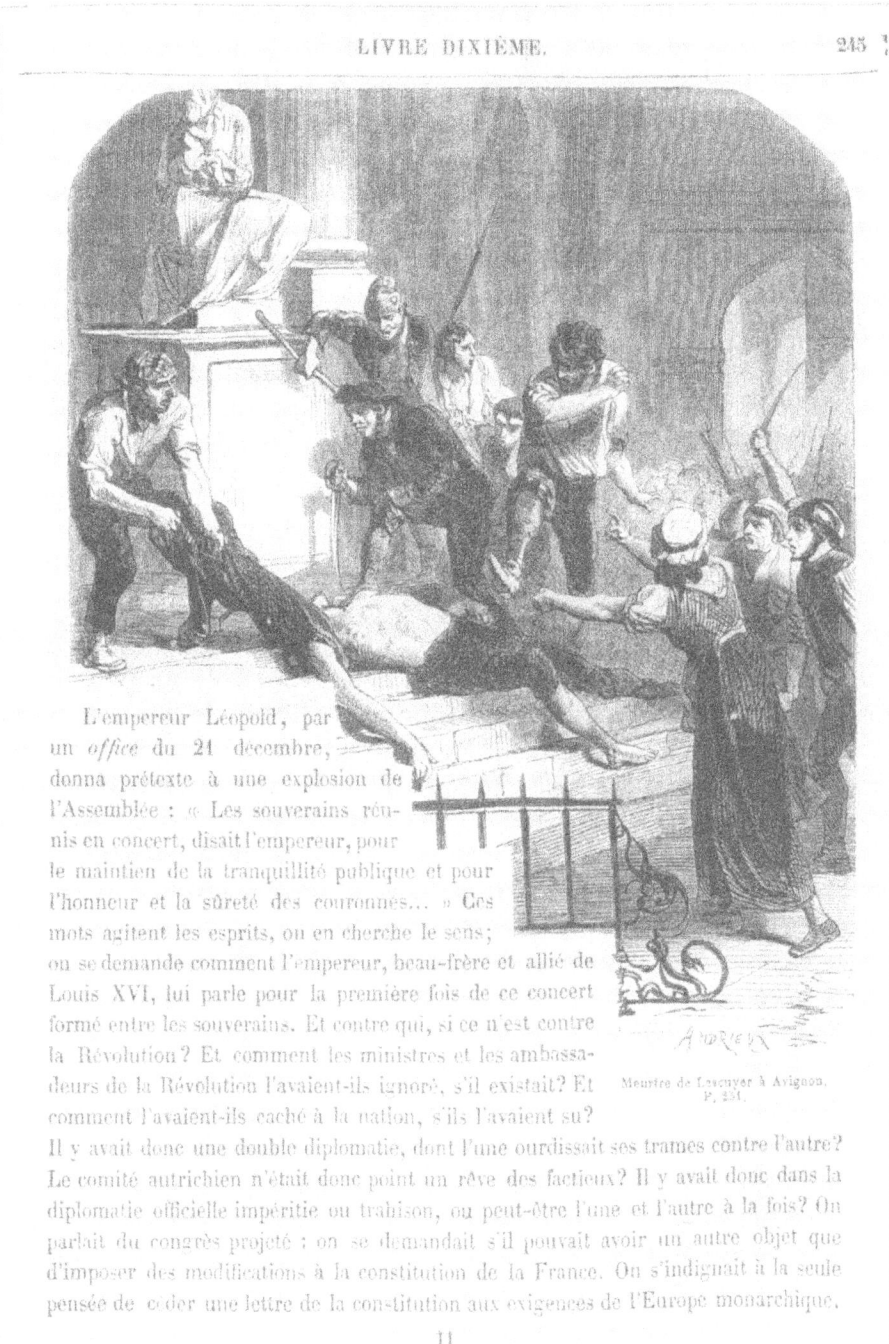

L'empereur Léopold, par un *office* du 24 décembre, donna prétexte à une explosion de l'Assemblée : « Les souverains réunis en concert, disait l'empereur, pour le maintien de la tranquillité publique et pour l'honneur et la sûreté des couronnes... » Ces mots agitent les esprits, on en cherche le sens; on se demande comment l'empereur, beau-frère et allié de Louis XVI, lui parle pour la première fois de ce concert formé entre les souverains. Et contre qui, si ce n'est contre la Révolution? Et comment les ministres et les ambassadeurs de la Révolution l'avaient-ils ignoré, s'il existait? Et comment l'avaient-ils caché à la nation, s'ils l'avaient su?

Meurtre de Lescuyer à Avignon.
P. 251.

Il y avait donc une double diplomatie, dont l'une ourdissait ses trames contre l'autre? Le comité autrichien n'était donc point un rêve des factieux? Il y avait donc dans la diplomatie officielle impéritie ou trahison, ou peut-être l'une et l'autre à la fois? On parlait du congrès projeté : on se demandait s'il pouvait avoir un autre objet que d'imposer des modifications à la constitution de la France. On s'indignait à la seule pensée de céder une lettre de la constitution aux exigences de l'Europe monarchique.

II

C'est dans cette émotion des esprits que le comité diplomatique, par l'organe du Girondin Gensonné, présenta son rapport sur l'état de nos relations avec l'empereur. Gensonné, avocat de Bordeaux, nommé à l'Assemblée législative le même jour que

FIGURE XXII Alphonse de Lamartine, *Histoire des Girondins*, 3 vols. (Paris: Armand Le Chevalier, 1865-1866), vol. 1, p. 245. Princeton University Library.

well-remembered artists,[138] all on separate unnumbered pages [figs. 206, 207]
An undated, two-volume edition in small print and double columns, continued in three further volumes to the Revolution of 1830 by Léonard Gallois
and published by Garnier, received the same treatment. The publisher of this
edition boasted that it was "ornée de cinquante gravures en taille-douce."
These copper-plate engravings were likewise printed on separate unnumbered pages [figs. 208–211]. For a new edition (Paris: Maresq et Cie and Gustave Havard) in 1851, however, the less expensive process of wood
engraving was chosen, and this allowed for copious illustrations to be
inserted in the text, as in the 1865 edition of Lamartine's *Histoire des
Girondins*, mentioned earlier [figs. 212–214]. A four-volume *Histoire populaire de la France* (Paris: Charles de Lahure, 1862–63) by Napoleon III's Education Minister, the prolific historian Victor Duruy, was "illustrée de 360
vignettes" in volume 1 alone. The same historian's *Histoire populaire contemporaine de la France*, also in four volumes (Paris: Hachette, 1864–65), carried
the story forward from 1815, where the previous work left off, and was likewise profusely illustrated, with 303 vignettes in the first volume alone. Illustrations also figured prominently in Duruy's numerous other historical
writings, which included several texts specifically intended for use in
schools[139] [figs. 215–224]. The title of Guizot's four-volume *L'Histoire de
France depuis les temps les plus reculés jusqu'en 1789 racontée à mes petits-
enfants* (Paris: Hachette, 1872–76) indicates clearly that the work was
directed not at an educated elite but at a new, far more numerous class of
readers, probably the same readers, female as well as male, who were avid
consumers of novels.[140] Like the histories of Thiers and Lamartine, it went
through many editions both in French and in English translation and was
profusely illustrated by currently successful artists—among them Alphonse
de Neuville who had illustrated the 1865–66 edition of Lamartine's *Histoire
des Girondins* [figs. 225–227]. As in the case of that edition of Lamartine and

[138]E.g. Napoléon Thomas, who exhibited work at the Salons of 1831–37, and Jules David
(1808–92), best known now for his popular fashion plates.

[139]E.g., *Histoire de l'Europe et de la France de 1270 à 1610* (Paris: Hachette, 1892), intended
for students in the "classe de seconde." The richness and technical proficiency of the illustrations in an 1879-1883 new edition of Duruy's frequently republished seven-volume *Histoire
des Romains, depuis les temps les plus reculés jusqu'à l'invasion des barbares* (Paris: Hachette;
1st ed. 1843–44), "enrichie d'environ 2500 gravures dessinées d'après l'antique et 100 cartes
et plans," suggests that there was also a market among the well-to-do for sumptuously illustrated books of history, or at least of ancient history and culture. The *Histoire des Romains*
was in part a work of archaeology, anthropology, and art history.

[140]The market aimed at, as well as the importance of illustrations to that market, is clearly
indicated by the title of one of the American editions—*A Popular History of France from the
Earliest Times*, translated by Robert Black, 6 vols. (Boston: Dana Estes and Charles E. Lauriat,
n.d. [1882])—and by the title-page of volume I, which boasted that that volume alone contained 340 illustrations. These, as in the original, were by Alphonse de Neuville. The *Histoire
d'Angleterre*, assembled by Guizot's daughter from her father's many writings on English history was similarly translated in the American editions as *A Popular History of England from
the Earliest Times to the Accession of Victoria* (Boston: Estes and Lauriat, 1876), while the English edition carried the title *The History of England from the Earliest Times to the Accession of
Queen Victoria related for the rising generation* (London: Sampson Low, Marston, Searle &
Rivington, 1877–79).

the 1851 edition of Anquetil, the 1861 edition of Norvins' *Histoire de Napoléon*, and the popular histories of Duruy, the illustrations were not high quality copper or steel engravings on separate pages but simpler (and cheaper) wood engravings printed on the same page as the text.

The publication of historical works in England and America followed a similar pattern to that in France. Early editions of the classic eighteenth-century histories of England by David Hume and his continuator Tobias Smollett, typically contained no illustrations. As in France, narratives of recent events and personalities were among the first to be illustrated. William Henry Ireland's four-volume *Life of Napoleon Bonaparte* (London: John Cumberland, 1823–38) and William Hamilton Maxwell's *History of the Irish Rebellion in 1798, with Memoirs of the Union and Emmett's Insurrection in 1803* (London: Baily Brothers, 1845) were both illustrated by Cruikshank.[141] Probably not coincindentally, both were the work of authors also known as writers of drama and fiction. At the end of the century, this tradition was maintained in the *Life of Wellington* by the Scottish novelist, historian, and conservative M.P. Sir Herbert Maxwell (London: S. Low, Marston, 1899) [fig. 228].

Illustrations also made an early appearance in histories intended for schools and young people. Oliver Goldsmith's *The History of England from the earliest times to the reign of George II* (London: T. Davies, 1771), "a shallow overview of English history" which "became an instant success as a schoolroom textbook," in the words of a modern editor of Jane Austen—who, as a young girl read and parodied Goldsmith's work[142]—was soon provided with a few illustrations of scenes such as "King John Signing Magna Carta" or "Wat Tyler Threatening Richard II." By the late 1840s, an American publisher had put out an edition continued "to the present time," "embellished with one hundred and seventy-three engravings," and thus quite appropriately retitled *Pictorial History of England* (Philadelphia: Thomas, Cowperthwait, 1849). The Abridgment prepared by Goldsmith himself in response to the huge success of his work (London: G. Kearsley, 1774) went through even more numerous editions and these were also often "embellished" with illustrations.[143] More popular still, especially in the United States,

---

[141]This was not, however, a universal rule. Southey's *Life of Nelson* (1813) and Scott's *Life of Bonaparte* (1827) contained no illustrations,

[142]Deirdre Le Faye, "A Note on the Text," in her facsimile edition of Austen's *The History of England from the Reign of Henry the 4th to the Death of Charles the 1st* (Chapel Hill: Algonquin Books, 1993), p. ix. Austen's hilarious little text, for which Cassandra drew charmingly witty miniature versions of the portraits of monarchs at the beginning of each chapter that were the sole acceptable illustrations in most histories of the seventeenth and eighteenth centuries, is a delightful anticipation of Sellar and Yeatman's justly celebrated *1066 and All That* (1930). The schoolroom use of Goldsmith is confirmed by the publisher's description of the French translation (1777) of Goldsmith's *History of England in a Series of Letters from a Nobleman to his Son* (1764) as "à l'usage des écoles."

[143]An advertisement at the end of *An Abridgement of the History of England from the Invasion of Julius Caesar to the Death of George the Second by Dr. Goldsmith, and continued by an eminent writer to the present period*, 12th ed. (London: W.J. and J. Richardson, R. Baldwin, F. and C. Rivington, 1805) for "the following popular School Books" (among them *Elements of Reading* and *Lectiones Selectae or Select Latin Lessons on Morality, History and Biography*) leaves no doubt as to the intended readership.

was *Pinnock's Improved Edition of Dr. Goldsmith's History of England from the Invasion of Julius Caesar to the Death of George II. With a continuation to the reign of George the Fourth; also a dictionary biographical, historical, &c. explaining every difficulty, and rendering the whole easy to be understood, and questions for examination at the end of each section* (London: G. and W.B. Whittaker, 1821). This work was printed in countless editions both in England and in America. One of the many editions of it put out by the Philadelphia publisher Cowperthwait—"the fifty-fifth American edition [1852], from the thirty-fifth English edition"—was correctly self-described as "illustrated with numerous engravings." As in the 1849 *Pictorial History*, the wood engravings in this edition, were not on separate pages but embedded in the text [figs. 229–231].

Goldsmith did not have the field entirely to himself. Hume's *History of England*, as continued by Smollett, was also abridged and adapted for school use. One such abridgment into a single octodecimo volume—*Hume and Smollett's celebrated History of England from its first Settlement to the Year 1760, accurately and impartially abridged, and a continuation to the Coronation of George IV, July 19, 1821*, ed. John Robinson (Hartford: F. Robinson, 1826)—boasted "24 pages of engravings," with two engravings to a page [fig. 232]. Also in America in the 1840s, the inexhaustibly prolific Samuel Goodrich, the author or co-author (often under the name Peter Palfrey) of countless books for the young, ranging from fictions to encyclopedias and dictionaries (of the Bible, of Botany, of History, of Commerce, etc.), brought out a series of small, single-volume "pictorial" histories: a *Pictorial History of France for Schools* (Philadelphia, 1842), a *Pictorial History of America for the use of schools* (Hartford, 1844), a *Pictorial History of England* (Philadelphia, 1845), a *Pictorial History of Greece, ancient and modern* (Philadelphia, 1846), and a *Pictorial History of Ancient Rome* (New York, 1849). As their titles imply, all these works for young people were profusely illustrated with wood engravings in the text. A larger, two-volume *History of all Nations from the earlier periods to the present time, or Universal History* (Boston, 1849–51), which purported to be both a history and a geography of the entire world and was printed in double columns to hold down costs, lacked the term "Pictorial" in the title. The title page, however, announced that the work was "illustrated by 70 stylographic maps and 700 engravings" [figs. 233–237].

Another market susceptible to the appeal of illustrations was created by the emergence in the nineteenth century of a new reading public of self-educated members of the working-class and *nouveaux-riches* middle-class merchants and entrepreneurs lacking the formal education of ministers, lawyers, and other professionals. By the 1830s, the practice of publishing contemporary fiction in illustrated editions, both in the final book form and in the separate "parts" that usually preceded it, was well established. Dickens' *Sketches by Boz* (1836) and *Oliver Twist* (1838) were illustrated by the celebrated cartoonist George Cruikshank, while Thackeray himself illustrated the parts and the first edition of *Vanity Fair* (1847–48) with steel and wood engravings averaging one to every three pages of text.[144] George Eliot's *Romola* (1862–63) was illustrated by no less an artist than Frederick Leighton. "Phiz" (Hablot Knight Browne) still enjoys a certain reputation as the illustrator of ten of Dickens' novels between 1836 and 1859, but Browne was kept busy, as were many other minor artists, illustrating the countless novels coming off the presses in the nineteenth century.[145] Even books of poetry were illustrated. An 1839 edition of Gray's "Elegy in a Country Churchyard," for instance, was illustrated by 23 artists, one of whom was John Constable. Illustrations also became a required feature of widely read magazines such as *Bentley's Miscellany* (1836), which serialized Dickens' *Oliver Twist*, the *Cornhill* (1860, with a starting circulation of 120,000 a month), and *Good Words* (also 1860), which appealed to a more popular audience. It has been shown that the unillustrated magazines of the early decades of the century either folded completely as the century advanced or saw their circulation decline significantly as they were replaced in the public favor by "a new type of magazine in which visual interest was prominent."[146] If historical narrative was to compete with fictional narrative for a share of the new mass market, publishers and authors must have reasoned, it too, would have to be as copiously illustrated as possible.[147]

Not surprisingly, histories produced as part of an earnest undertaking to "improve" society by educating the new class of readers were particularly likely to be illustrated. One of the earliest of these—the eight–volume *Pictorial History of England, being a history of the people, as well as a history of the kingdom* by George Lillie Craik and Charles MacFarlane (London: Charles Knight, 1838–44)—was a collaborative project directed and edited by a Scot (Craik) who had been caught up in the work of the Society for the Diffusion of Useful Knowledge. The aim of the Society, established in 1825

---

[144]Christopher Coates, "Thackeray's editors and the text of *Vanity Fair*," *Word and Image*, 9 (1993): 39–50.

[145]Stuart Sillars, *Visualisation in Popular Fiction 1860-1960*, pp. 10–17; see also, on illustrations of nineteenth-century novels, Percy Muir, *Victorian Illustrated Books* (London: Batsford, 1971); Geoffrey Wakeman, *Victorian Book Illustration* (1974); and, especially on periodical magazines, Paul Goldman, *Victorian Illustrated Books* (1994), pp. 48–64. Richard Altick defines the criteria for the successful popular magazine as "a price of 6d or lower; plenty of light fiction and amusing non-fiction; and as many illustrations as possible." (*The English Common Reader: A Social History of the Mass Reading Public* [Chicago: University of Chicago Press, 1957]. p. 363)

[146]Sillars, *Visualisation in Popular Fiction*, pp. 72–74. Thus, among literary magazines, *Blackwood's*, which began publication in 1817, saw its circulation drop from 10,000 to 3,000 after the appearance of the *Cornhill* in 1860. According to Altick, "a generous supply of pictures became an almost indispensable adjunct to text in the journals that sought to exploit the working-class market." (*The English Common Reader*, p. 344)

[147]Curiously, Dickens' own foray into popular history, *A Child's History of England*, published serially, starting in 1851, in his weekly magazine *Household Words* and in book form in 1854, was not illustrated, nor was the first American edition published the following year by Harper Brothers in New York. The deficiency was quickly made up, however, in the Illustrated Library Edition of 1861-1874 and in the many subsequent editions published in the United States [figs. 238–241]. The editions published in Boston by Estes and Lauriat (1873,1881 and 1886), for instance, included first 24, then 100 full-page illustrations in some 470 pages of text.

at the instigation of the influential, Edinburgh-born liberal reformer and abolitionist Henry, Lord Brougham, was to spread education among working and lower-middle-class people who had not had the benefit of formal schooling (and thus doubtless also to keep them from being drawn toward dangerously radical associations and ideologies). Craik and MacFarlane's *Pictorial History* reflected the aims and the views of the Society and its founders. It focused less than the French historians we have discussed on wars, revolutions, the grand and heroic actions of remarkable individuals and popular masses, and stood closer to history as the historians of the Enlightenment had envisaged it, more or less equal sections being devoted, for each period, not only to "civil and military transactions" (i.e. affairs of state, international affairs, and wars) but to the "history of religion," "industry," " the constitution, government, and laws," "literature," "science and the fine arts," "manners and customs," and the "condition of the people." To enhance its appeal to its targeted audience, it used the same method as the Society's popular *Penny Magazine* and, as the title page announced, was "illustrated with many hundred wood-cuts"—400 or so in the first volume alone. But in accordance with its declared focus on other aspects of the past besides political and military history, the illustrations were "of monumental records, coins, civil and military costume, domestic buildings, furniture and ornaments; cathedrals and other great works of architecture; sports and other illustrations of manners; mechanical inventions; portraits of the kings and queens; their signatures and great seals." "Remarkable historical scenes" came last on this list[148] and illustrations of them—mostly wood engravings based on drawings or paintings by successful contemporary or recent artists, such as James Northcote (1746–1831) and Thomas Stothard (1755–1834)—are in fact far outnumbered, especially in the early volumes by illustrations featuring artifacts of the time being described. Craik thus integrated into the *Pictorial History* a type of illustration that was more commonly employed in works by seventeenth-, eighteenth-, and nineteenth-century antiquarians and archeologists, such as Layard's magnificent *Discoveries in the Ruins of Nineveh and Babylon* (London: John Murray, 1853), inasmuch as these offered descriptions of artifacts, states of culture or civilization, and conditions of life, rather than narratives of events and actions [figs. 242–246]. A note at the end of the list of illustrations in volume 1 clarifies the editor's view of the nature and purpose of the illustrations. "It is to be understood that the Wood-cuts have in general been copied from drawings, sculptures, coins, or other works of the period which they are employed to illustrate; but [. . .] it sometimes happened that no suitable illustration of the custom or other matter described was to be found among the remains of the period under consideration; in a few such cases a drawing from a subsequent period has been made use of where there was reason to believe that it nevertheless conveyed a sufficiently accurate representation of the thing spoken of. [. . .] The copies of modern historical pictures, it will of course be under-

---

[148]The list appears on the title page of vol. 5 (1841).

stood, have been given for other reasons altogether than their fidelity in regard to costume and other characteristics." In the majority of cases, in short, the illustrations are based on the most authentic available artifacts of the time and these are distinguished from illustrations by modern artists, the purpose of which is not to give a faithful representation of the past, but to stimulate the reader's imagination [figs. 247–249].

Being published first, like the novels of the time, in monthly "parts" (beginning in 1837), the *Pictorial History* was a considerable success, though the last volumes, which were devoted to the reign of George III and were less liberal in tone, appear to have sold less well. An updated and abridged—but unillustrated—version, based on MacFarlane's contribution (i.e., the sections on "civil and military transactions") appeared as *The Cabinet History of England* in 1845-46 with the same publisher, Charles Knight, and in new editions in 1856–61 and 1876–78. Another version of this abridgment, retitled *The Comprehensive History of England*, "illustrated by above one thousand engravings," was published in four volumes from 1856 to 1861 and again in 1876–78. Finally, a three-volume version with yet another title, *The Popular History of England*, appeared as late as 1886.

The publisher of the *Pictorial History*, Charles Knight, an enterprising political reformer and popularizer of literature, art, and science in his own right, was also closely associated with the Society for the Diffusion of Useful Knowledge and in 1832, the year of the great Reform Bill, had launched the *Penny Magazine* as the Society's official organ. Aimed at working class and lower middle-class readers with a modicum of education and a desire for more, this earliest of the popular illustrated magazines of the nineteenth century is said to have attained a circulation of 200,000 in its heyday.[149] Knight also turned out the *Penny Cyclopedia of the Society for the Diffusion of Useful Knowledge* (27 volumes, 1833–44), *The Pictorial Bible* (1836–38), and *The Pictorial Shakespeare* (1839–42), to mention only a few of the numerous projects he instigated and helped to realize. Two decades after publishing the history of Craik and MacFarlane in its first version, Knight himself produced an eight-volume *Popular History of England*, which he described in terms strongly reminiscent of those used by Craik, as "a History of the People as well as a History of the State."[150] Knight himself identified

---

[149]See Richard Altick, *The English Common Reader*, p. 335. The *Illustrated London News* began life in 1842, *L'Illustration* in Paris in 1843.

[150]Charles Knight, *The Popular History of England. An Illustrated History of Society and Government from the Earliest Period to our Own Times*, 8 vols. (London: Bradbury and Evans, 1856-62), vol. 8, p. iii. A second edition, also in 8 vols. and virtually identical with the first, began appearing in 1862 (London: James Sangster and Co.); an American edition, again in 8 vols., but differently and far less profusely illustrated, was published in New York (John Wurtele Lovell) in 1880; altogether there were ten editions between 1854 and 1890. An abridged edition for schools (one volume of 912 pp.) appeared in 1865 under the title *A School History of England* (London: Bradbury and Evans). Knight's view was that history should not be either domestic or public, either about society and "civilization" or about the state and politics, but should combine both, for "we should understand the inseparable connection between the State history and the Domestic. [. . .] We must look at history from a new

the public for which it was intended as one situated between the schoolboy readers of "potted" versions of Goldsmith on the one hand and the reflective, leisured class of well-educated readers of Hume on the other. His *Popular History* was addressed, he explained, to the "'young man of eighteen'"—i.e., to a reader who was no longer an immature schoolboy but "representative of a very large class of readers in the present day." This class of readers, Knight specified, is made up of "those, of either sex, who with the average amount of intelligence that has now made us a reading people, have no superabundant leisure for pursuing the history of their country as a laborious and difficult study." Granted that "the lawyer and the statesman cannot be satisfied with a compendious history, [. . .] for the great body of present day readers twenty octavo volumes constitute a formidable undertaking." Hence, what is needed in the "new age" is "a *compendious* work [italics in text], written upon a uniform plan"—that is to say, not an abridged or watered down version of a longer, more complete work, such as Hume's, but a work specifically designed for the new class of readers—"[. . .] a History that should hold a middle place, as to its extent, between the school-history, such as that of Goldsmith, and the library-history of Hume."[151] Knight's history was not only to be "compendious" enough to be read by "the great body of present day readers," it was to appeal to them by means of abundant illustrations—some full-page steel engravings (portraits of kings in the early volumes and composite portraits of eminent statesmen, writers, painters, explorers, and scientists, in the later volumes), but mostly vignettes printed on the same page as the text, using the relatively inexpensive wood engraving process also employed by Craik, as well as the *Penny Magazine*. The first volume alone had eight "portraits on steel" and 305 wood engravings illustrating not only notable events and actions but, as in Craik's *Pictorial History*, places, people, and working and living conditions [figs. XXIII, 250–254]. It is noteworthy that at this early stage Knight, like Craik, was already illustrating his text not only with works by modern artists depicting dramatic scenes from the past, but with images of artifacts (coins, seals, sculptures, architecture) and drawings based on manuscript illuminations and old engravings from the time about which he was writing.

Knight's *History* was itself followed within a year by *Cassell's Illustrated History of England* (1857–1860), which the publisher John Cassell, whose

---

point of view. We must put the People in the foreground. We must study events and institutions, not as abstract facts, but as influencing the condition of a whole nation." The People, moreover, toward whom the *Popular History* is directed, is not to be defined as "any distinct class or section of the population." Goldsmith's definition of the People as "the middle order of mankind," as distinct from "those below them, the 'Rabble'," is rejected. "We have outlived all this. A century of thought and action has widened and deepened the foundations of the State"—and also thereby the readership envisaged for the *Popular History*. (*The Popular History of England*, vol. 1, Introduction, pp. iii-iv) See also Knight's account of his work and of how he understood it to be different from the work of Craik and MacFarlane—which he describes as "in many respects a valuable history, but one whose limits had gone far beyond what, as its projector, I had originally contemplated." (*Passages from the Life of Charles Knight* [New York: G.P. Putnam's Sons, 1874], p. 464)

[151] *The Popular History of England*, vol. 1, Introduction, pp. 1–11.

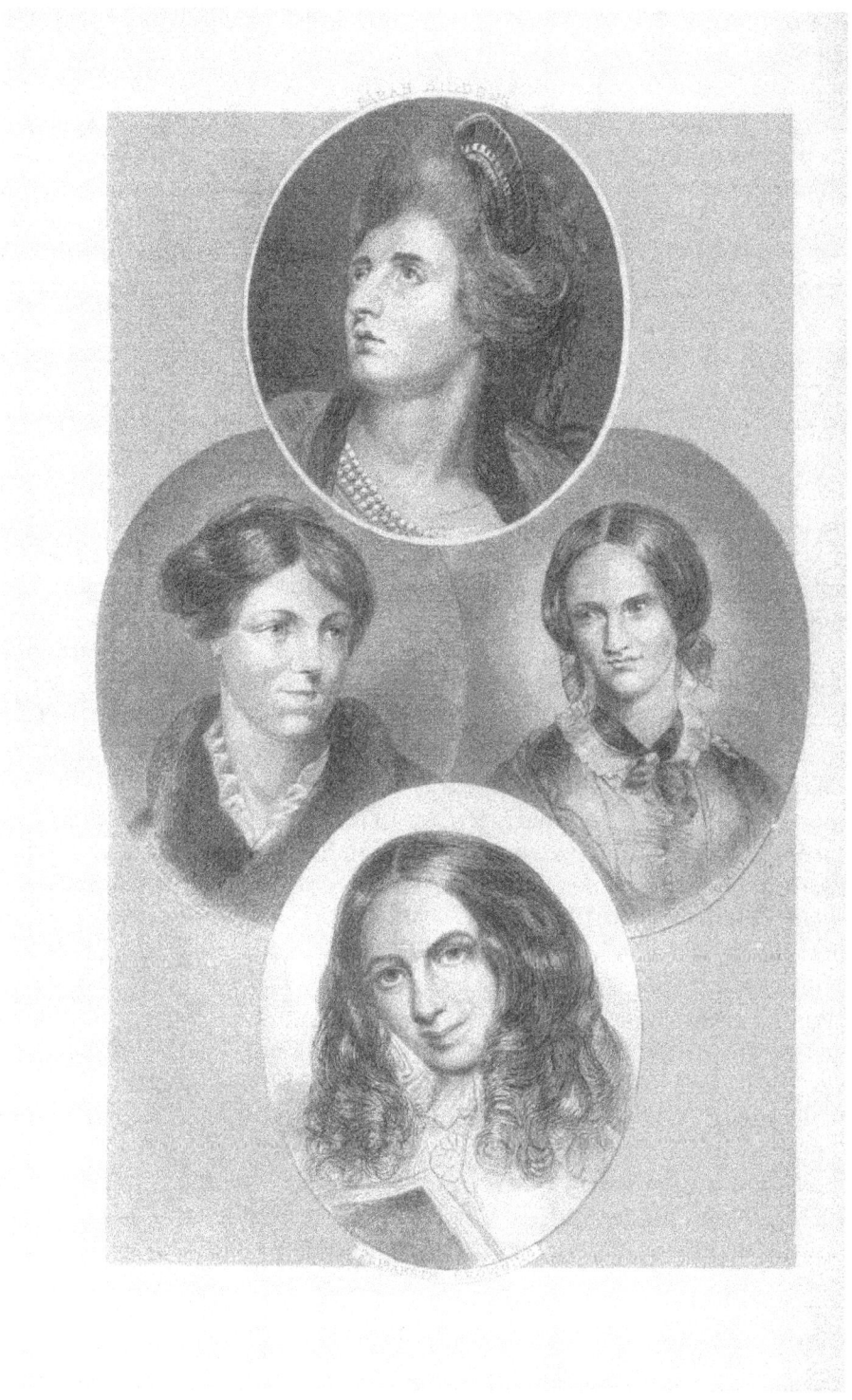

FIGURE **XXIII** Composite portrait of Sarah Siddons, Harriet Martineau, Charlotte Bronte, and Elizabeth Browning in Charles Knight, *Popular History of England*, 8 vols. (London: Bradbury and Evans, 1856-1862), vol. 8, facing p. 481. Princeton University Library.

main purpose in life was "giving Literature and Education to the People at the lowest cost,"[152] commissioned from William Howitt, the author of several highly successful popular books, such as *The Book of the Seasons* and *A Popular History of Priestcraft*.[153] To hold down the price, this work, like Craik's, was printed in double columns, and to make it attractive to as broad a public as possible, it was illustrated with numerous wood engravings, both full page and in the text (over 150 in the first volume alone). The publisher's strategy appears to have worked well, for *Cassell's Illustrated History* sold over a quarter of a million copies and was republished many times in updated and revised editions right into the twentieth century [figs. XXIV, 255–262].[154] Following the pattern set by Craik and Knight, it covered not only politics and wars but social conflicts, the arts and sciences, and customs and fashions, to which it added major events in foreign countries. The *Popular History of England*, put together by Guizot's daughter from the statesman-historian's many works on English history, enjoyed similar success and was likewise profusely illustrated [figs. 263–266].

German historiographical publications seem to have followed a broadly similar path to that taken in France and England. Scholarly histories, based on original research and reflection, such as those of Ranke and Droysen, were not illustrated. Even many general histories contained no illustrations. It seems to have mattered little whether they were intended "für alle Stände" [for all social ranks], as many proclaimed in their titles, "für gebildete Leser" [for educated readers] as some also announced, or for "denkende Geschichtsfreunde" [reflective lovers of history], as was specified on the title page of one edition (Freiburg: Herder, 1832–34) of the constantly updated, revised, reprinted, and widely translated, multi-volume universal history— *Allgemeine Geschichte vom Anfang der historischen Kenntnis bis auf unsere Zeiten* (1st ed. 1803–1818)—by Carl von Rotteck, a liberal statesman-scholar from Baden in South Germany.[155] Even Johann Matthias Schröckh's eighteenth-century *Allgemeine Weltgeschichte für Kinder* [General History for Children], re-edited several times in the first half of the nineteenth century, was not illustrated. Nor was a self-proclaimed "inexpensive edition" of an *Allgemeine Weltgeschichte: Lehr- und Lesebuch für das deutsche Volk* [General Universal History: A Manual of Instruction for the German People] (Kempton: Tobias Dannheimer, 1846).

Around mid-century, however, there appears to have been a trend, which gathered momentum as the century advanced, to include illustrations in histories aimed at a broader market. An 1848 edition of Rotteck, pub-

---

[152]Newman Flower, *Just as it Happened* (New York: William Morrow, 1950), p. 50. On Cassell, see Ch. V, pp. 50-59. Cassell himself told Richard Cobden that he had always striven for "something higher than commercial success, namely [. . .] the moral and intellectual advancement of the people." (Cit. ibid., p. 58)

[153]Volume 1, on the earliest period, was by J.F. Smith. Howitt was the author of all the others.

[154]Newman Flower, *Just as it Happened*, p. 55.

[155]According to the Preface of a new four-volume American edition of Rotteck's *History* in English translation (Philadelphia: Leary and Getz, 1856): "100,000 copies (in various editions and forms) have been sold within a few years" in Germany alone. (Preface, p. vi)

reached in their turn; probably trembling for the conse-quences of their daring conduct, on seeing Darnley and the queen reconciled, they consented, and in the night the queen and Darnley mounted fleet horses and fled to Dunbar. The consternation of the murderers, in the morning, may be imagined. The outraged and insulted queen had escaped their hands, and the news came flying that already the nobles

treason and bloodshed, rushed away to conceal himself in the fastness of Kyle. Maitland of Lethington betook him-self to the hills of Atholl, and Craig, the colleague of Knox, dived into the darksome recesses of the city wynds.

Mary, once more free, resumed all the decision of her character. But she had a difficult part to play. Willing to think the best, and only too prone to forgive, she yet

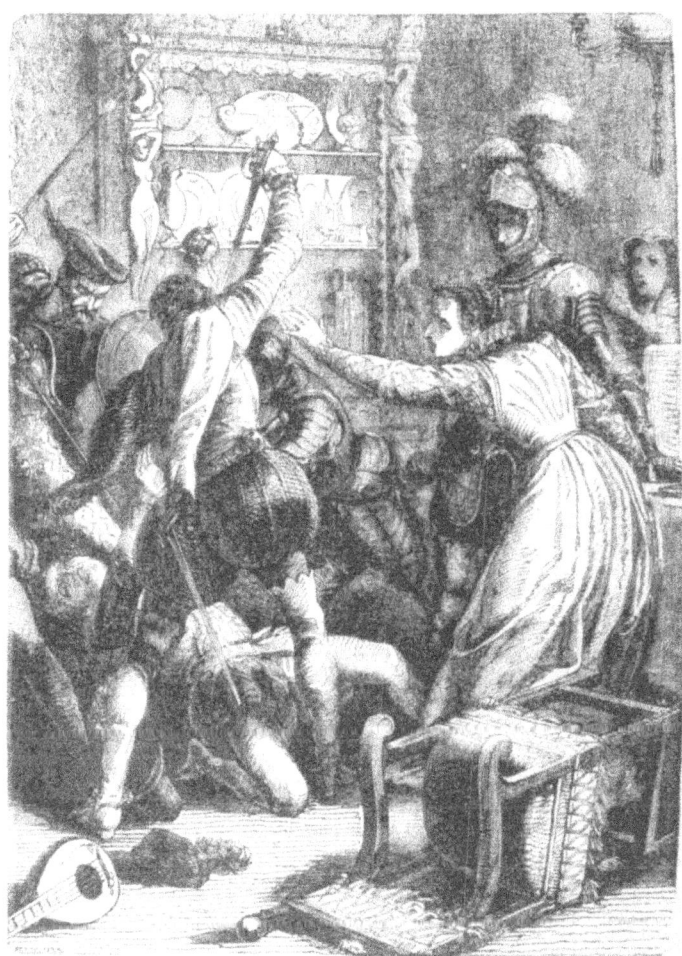

Murder of Rizzio   See page 431.

and the people were hurrying from all sides to her standard. Huntley, Atholl, Bothwell, and whole crowds of barons and gentlemen, flew to her, and at Dunbar a numerous army stood as by magic ready to march on the traitors and execute the vengence due. They fled. Morton, Ruthven, the grisly, pale-faced assassin, Brunston, and Car of Faulbouside escaped to England, and Knox, the apostle of

must have seen enough to shake her faith in all around her Darnley, spite of his protestation, had appeared simulta-neously with the assassins, and what had been the real con-duct of Murray ? Besides the doubts which hung around many of her courtiers, they were almost all at deadly feud with each other. There was nothing for it, however, but to make the best of her materials. She reconciled Both-

FIGURE XXIV   "Murder of Rizzio" in William Howitt, *John Cassell's Illustrated History of England*, 8 vols., vol. 2, "From the Reign of Edward IV to the Death of Queen Elizabeth, with upwards of three hundred engravings" (London: Kent and Co., 1858), p. 432. Princeton University Library.

lished in Braunschweig announced that it contained "26 original steel engravings."[156] A later edition "für alle Stände" (Stuttgart: Rieger, 1869–70), updated by Wilhelm Zimmermann—an outspokenly left-leaning theologian, delegate to the 1848 Frankfurt Parliament, and prolific author of popular historical works of his own—was also illustrated [figs. 267, 268], as were numerous other mid-nineteenth century updatings and translations of Rotteck. For his own *Illustrirte Geschichte des deutschen Volkes* ["Illustrated History of the German People"] (Stuttgart: Rieger, 1873–77)—Zimmermann and his publisher engaged the services of Friedrich Hottenroth (1840–1917) an illustrator of the time well known for his studies of ancient and modern costume. The English translation of this work, which followed the publication of the original German almost immediately and was doubtless aimed at the large American population of German descent (New York: Henry J. Johnson, n.d. [1877]), bore the title *A Popular History of Germany from the earliest period to the present day, with over 600 illustrations by eminent German artists.* These illustrations, both full-page engravings and wood engravings in the text, were intended to offer vivid visual representations of the actions and episodes recounted in the narrative, such as "Belleisle's Retreat from Prague" or "Götz of the Iron Hand in the Camp of the Insurgents" [figs. XXV, 269–271], as were the images in Otto Kaemmel's *Deutsche Geschichte* (Dresden: Holckner, 1889), which acquired more and more illustrations as it went through edition after edition. There were no fewer than 263 in volume I of the third edition (Leipzig: Otto Spamer, 1911) [figs. 272, 273]. Dramatic incidents and scenes—such as "Victory at Leipzig" or "Friedrich Wilhelm IV of Prussia grants the Constitution, 6 February, 1850"—are likewise the subjects of images in the appropriate volume of *Spamer's illustrierte Weltgeschichte mit zahlreichen Textabbildungen, Kunstbeilagen und Karten* (1893–98), a multi-volume universal history edited by Kaemmel and aimed at a broad market, the earlier volumes of which, however, dealing with ancient and non-European societies, are strongly focused on cultural history.

As rapidly improving literacy rates in Western European countries and in the United States in the course of the nineteenth century broadened the market for books beyond the old upper-middle-class and as "public interest in the pictorial increased" in all classes,[157] more and more of the great classics of historiography also began to appear in illustrated, sometimes abridged editions. In editions of 1804 (Philadelphia), 1827 (Oxford), and 1854 (London), Gibbon's *Decline and Fall* was not illustrated, but by the end of the nineteenth century and the beginning of the twentieth illustrations of buildings, sarcophagi, and other ancient artifacts, as well as scenes and episodes,

---

[156]This was probably not the earliest illustrated edition of Rotteck. As the first American translation and continuation—to 1840—(Philadelphia: C. F. Stollmeyer, 1840–41, 4 vols.) was "illustrated by twenty-four historical engravings," it is extremely likely that these engravings were taken over from the German edition on which the translation was based.

[157]According to Newman Flower, who ran the publishing house of Cassell for many years until the end of Word War II, demand for the pictorial intensified as a result of the Great Exhibition of 1851. (*Just as it Happened*, p. 71)

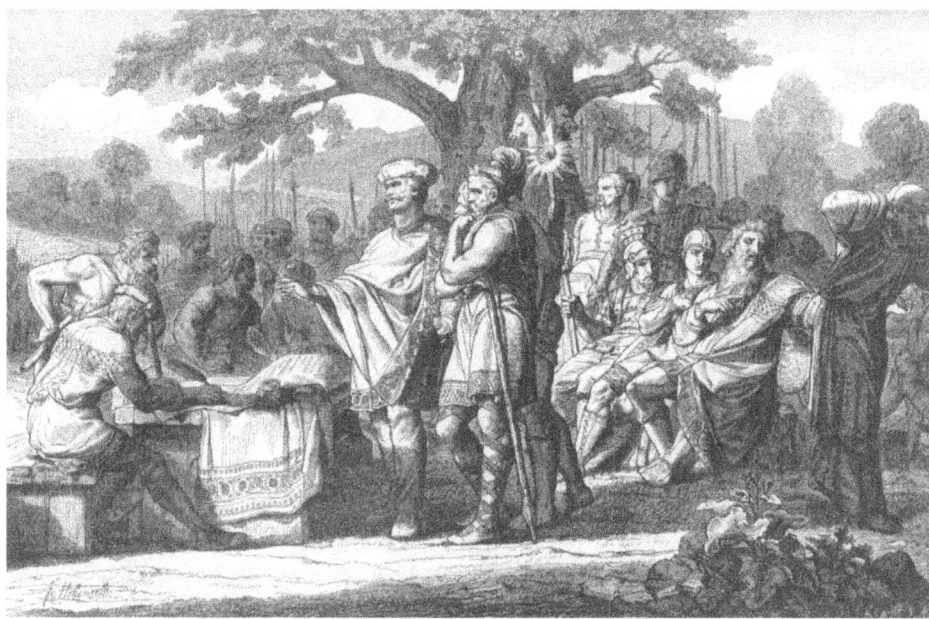

FIGURE XXV Friedrich Hottenroth, "Confirmation of the Liberties of the Ripuarian Franks," in Wilhelm Zimmermann, *A Popular History of Germany from the Earliest Period to the Present Day*, 4 vols. (New York: Henry J. Johnson, n.d. [1877]; orig. German 1873-1877), vol. 2, between pp. 634 and 635. Princeton University Library.

had begun to make their appearance[158] [fig. 274]. In its frequently republished English translation, Ranke's *History of the Popes* was generally not illustrated.[159] A 1901 edition, however, in "The World's Great Classics Series" (New York and London: Colonial Press), boasted that it was "illustrated with nearly three hundred photogravures, etchings, colored plates and full page portraits." The early editions of Michelet's *Histoire de France* (1st ed., 17 volumes, Paris: Hachette, then Chamerot, 1833–67) and of his *Histoire de la Révolution française* (1st ed., 7 volumes, Paris: Chamerot, 1847–53) were similarly devoid of illustrations, despite the historian's keen interest in the visual arts. By the late 1890s, however, most of the 19 volumes of the *Histoire de France* in the *Oeuvres complètes* published by Calmann-Lévy (1898–99)

[158]Still sparingly, for example, in a 1914 edition (New York: Macmillan), the seven volumes of which contained 20 illustrations and two maps; more copiously and expensively (all illustrations were printed on separate pages and in two copies, one of which was sometimes in color) in a fifteen-volume "Conoisseur edition" of *Gibbon's Complete Works* (New York: De Fau, n.d. [1906–07]).

[159]E.g,, London: John Murray, 1866; London: George Bell [later Bell and Sons], 1876, 1896, 1913. An 1846 edition, entitled *The Popes of Rome*, put out by the progressive Glasgow publisher Blackie, did, however, contain a number of portrait engravings by the then popular engraver Henry Robinson. In a few cases the engraving is after an original painting (by Titian or Velasquez) but mostly Robinson's name appears alone. It is likely, therefore, that the majority of the illustrations were original works by him. Compulsory primary education had been established in Scotland in the early seventeenth century and the records of the earliest public libraries demonstrate the popularity of works on religious topics. Blackie could thus have been aiming at a quite broad public.

were adorned with a few portraits by artists more or less contemporary with their subjects, such as Clouet, Fouquet, Philippe de Champaigne, and Van Dyck.[160] As for the *Histoire de la Révolution* in the Calmann-Lévy edition, every volume announced on the title page that it came "avec gravures d'après des documents historiques"—usually three or four portraits or engravings of the time. Even in its fourth edition (Paris: Furne 1865), the sixteen-volume *Histoire de France depuis les temps les plus reculés jusqu'en 1789* by Michelet's rival Henri Martin, was not illustrated; fourteen years later, in contrast, the same author's four-volume *Histoire de France depuis 1789 jusqu'à nos jours,* with the same publisher, contained portraits and several engravings of scenes [figs. 275, 276].

The illustration of history books was affected not only by the emergence of a new class of readers but by a concomitant reorientation of a substantial part of historiography toward cultural history, the history of "ordinary people," of society, as distinct from the history of the state and its leaders. The use by Craik, Knight, and others of images representing coins, seals, manuscript illuminations, old buildings and landscapes, costumes and furnishings from the period under discussion has already been noted. Largely forgotten now, the abundant *oeuvre* (over forty popular works of history, art history and art criticism) of Armand Dayot, *inspecteur général* in the Ministry of Fine Arts after the establishment of the French Third Republic, merits special attention here because of Dayot's deliberate embrace of the image as the primary element of his historiography, rather than an accessory to the text. His goal of a history "raconté par l'image"[161] went beyond anything imagined by Craik or Knight. For Dayot, as an art historian, the illustration came first and the textual narrative was dependent on it. His books thus look forward to some popular publications of recent times, such as the American Heritage Publishing Company's *Horizon Book* series.[162] Above all, the function of the image in Dayot's work was not simply representational, as in most of the writings of the antiquarians and earlier historians; it was not simply to convey the external appearance of things or people and back up a verbal description. It was also expressive. In and of itself, as conceived by Dayot, the image bore witness to the culture—the outlook, feelings, ideas— of those who had produced it and of the time in which they lived. Raffet's *Musée de la Révolution* (1834), mentioned earlier, had also been composed of images created by contemporaries or near-contemporaries, if not actual eyewitnesses. As it was published while the events depicted in it were still fresh in living memory, however, it was more like an extended set of broadsheets or *Bilderbogen,* more a chronicle than a history—in the sense that

---

[160]Exceptionally, Joan of Arc was represented by Ingres' famous painting of her at the Coronation of Charles VII.

[161]From the title of one of Dayot's works, *Napoléon raconté par l'image, d'après les sculpteurs, les graveurs et les peintres* (1895).

[162]Among them: *The Renaissance* (by J.H. Plumb, 1961), *The Age of Napoleon* (by J. Christopher Herold, 1963), *Ancient Rome* (by Robert Payne, 1966), *The Elizabethan World* (by Lacey Baldwin Smith, 1967).

chronicle has the character of an eyewitness report, whereas history is a reconstructed account of situations and events from which writer and reader have been significantly distanced by the passage of time. Moreover, as noted, Raffet's *Musée* not only consisted largely of representations of major actions and actors, it did not claim to be itself a history of the Revolution; it claimed only to complement or illustrate any verbal narrative history. In contrast, the aim of Dayot's *La Révolution française (Constituante—Législative—Convention—Directoire) d'après des Peintures, Sculptures, Gravures, Médailles, Objets [. . .] du Temps*, published in 1896, a century after the events that are its subject, was to offer "une narration rapide, vivante, sincère, peuplée de documents artistiques, empruntés à cette époque mémorable"—that is to say, a history constructed from images and documents of the time, rather than a verbal narrative enlivened by modern illustrations or by illustrations whose representational authenticity was guaranteed by their having been created at the time they were being used to illustrate. Moreover, the images in Dayot included facsimile reproductions of signed documents, handwritten letters, banknotes, and similar everyday items. Since this formula had worked successfully in his *Napoléon raconté par l'image*, published by Hachette in the previous year, Dayot was confident that it would again prove attractive to a large number of readers [figs. XXVI, 277–281].[163]

While the story that has to be told, he concedes, unlike that in the book on Napoleon, is not the gripping story of an extraordinary individual, it is no less "varié, pittoresque et saisissant," for its topic is "the pulsating life of a whole people out of which emerge each day, like flashes of lightning in a storm, figures both sinister and sublime, both among the victors and among the vanquished."[164] Even though his hero is now an entire nation rather than an extraordinary individual, in short, Dayot still emphasizes the narrative aspect of his work, the striking particular actions, actors, and tumultuous events ("flashes of lightning") characterized later by Fernand Braudel as a "fireworks display" that fails to pierce the night of the past "with any true

---

[163]A. Dayot, *La Révolution française (Constituante—Législative—Convention—Directoire) d'après des Peintures, Sculptures, Gravures, Médailles, Objets [. . .] du Temps* (Paris: Ernest Flammarion, n.d. [1896], Preface). Dayot went on to publish, in addition to many works of art history and art criticism, *Journées révolutionnaires 1830-1848 d'après des peintures, gravures, sculptures, dessins, médailles, objets [. . .] du temps* (Paris: Ernest Flammarion, n.d. [1897]); *La Restauration (Louis XVIII - Charles X) d'après l'image du temps* (Paris: La Revue blanche, 1902); *Le Moyen Age, la Gaule romaine, les Invasions, la France féodale, la Royauté* (Paris: Ernest Flammarion, n.d.); *Le Second Empire, 2 décembre 1851–4 septembre 1870 d'après des peintures, gravures, photographies, sculptures, dessins, médailles autographes, objets du temps* (Paris: Ernest Flammarion, 1900); *Histoire contemporaine par l'image, d'après les documents du temps 1789-1872* (Paris: Ernest Flammarion, 1905); *L'Invasion, le Siège, la Commune 1870-1871, d'après des peintures, gravures, photographies, sculptures, médailles autographes, objets du temps* (Paris: Ernest Flammarion, n.d. [1901]), *De la Régence à la Révolution. La Vie française au XVIIIème siècle* (Paris: Ernest Flammarion, 1906); *L'Image de la femme depuis l'antiquité jusqu'à nos jours* (Paris: Hachette,1899).

[164]"la vie frémissante de tout un people . . . d'où surgissent chaque jour, comme jaillissent les éclairs de la tempête, des figures sinistres et sublimes, qu'il s'agisse des vainqueurs ou des vaincus." (Preface)

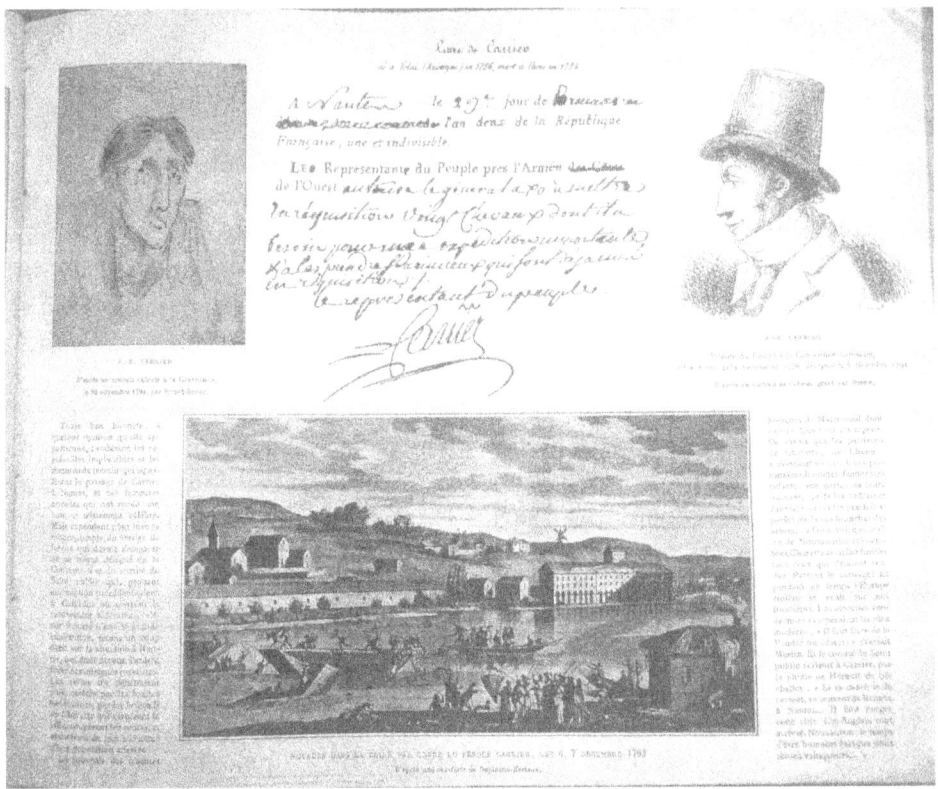

FIGURE XXVI Armand Dayot, *La Révolution Française; Constituante, Législative, Convention, Directoire, d'après des Peintures, Sculptures, Gravures, Médailles, Objets du Temps* (Paris: Flammarion, 1896), p. 311.

illumination."[165] In his emphasis on narrative, Dayot remains conventional. At the same time, however, his considered decision to use only documentary images and images created by eyewitnesses rather than images created by later artists, and, above all, to have those images speak directly to the reader rather than simply illustrate a particular point in a preexisting verbal text broke new ground, as he himself explicitly claimed, in the way images were used in historiography.

Dayot noted three benefits of his strategy. First, readers would be brought to re-experience the past through direct "contact avec les faits du passé," that is, through direct contact with the living sources (documents and contemporary pictorial representations) "où sont venus puiser les plus grands historiens" ["drawn upon by the greatest historians"]. Second, by dispensing with the mediation of historians—"les Mignet, les Cabet, les Michelet, les Thiers,"—readers of his book would obtain a truly "impartial," truly objective view of the past. Dayot emphasized that many of the images in his book, "dans leur facture cursive et sommaire, ont toute la sincérité des instantanés photographiques." In this respect, he implied, they offered a path beyond even literary realism to the real itself, just as the photograph supposedly provided

---

[165]Braudel, *Ecrits sur l'histoire* (Paris: Flammarion, 1969), p. 22.

an unmediated view that not even the most realistic painting could match. Justifying the brevity of his own verbal commentaries, Dayot explained that his primary aim was to "raconter impartialement par l'image le gigantesque drame." The image, in other words, speaks for itself. Third, Dayot made the somewhat paradoxical but by no means contradictory claim that the strategy he had adopted had enabled him to write a book that was both about historical events and personalities and about the art in which those events and personalities had been represented. The art itself, in short, no less in its form than its content, functioned as historical testimony. The *signifiant*, in the language of linguistics, was as relevant to history as the *signifié*:

> Cette publication, tout en demeurant une sorte de journal illustré de la grande époque révolutionnaire, d'après les pièces du temps, une sorte de récit par l'image des événements qui se sont écoulés depuis le 1er mai 1789 jusqu'au 9 novembre 1799 (18 brumaire), se présente aussi comme un recueil très artistique, où, à côté d'estampes d'une exécution aussi sincère que naïve, et d'objets familiers d'une incontestable authenticité, apparaissent des chefs d'oeuvre dans l'exécution desquels on pourra reconnaître à la fois la vérité de l'histoire et l'art de la fin du siècle passé.[166]

Dayot's goal of a history "raconté par l'image" with only minimal use of verbal text may well have been exceptional; however, his considered use of images not just to enliven or facilitate the reading of a text but to serve in

---

[166]"While it is at all times a kind of illustrated journal of the great revolutionary age as seen through the objects and documents of the time, a kind of narrative in pictures of the events that took place between May 1, 1789 and November 9, 1799 (the 18th Brumaire), this publication also serves as a highly artistic collection in which, alongside sincerely and naively produced prints and indisputably authentic everyday objects, the reader will find masterpieces in the execution of which are displayed both the truth of history and the art of the past century." (Armand Dayot, *La Révolution française (Constituante—Législative—Convention—Directoire) d'après des Peintures, Sculptures, Gravures, Médailles, Objets [. . .] du Temps* [Paris: Ernest Flammarion, n.d. (1896)], préface, pp. 1–3) Though images dominate text in Dayot's historical works, they are arranged chronologically around successive public actions and events. The overall design of the works thus continues to be determined by a political narrative. In purely cultural histories, the political played a less prominent role and the design was not primarily narrative; e.g. *Der Wiener Congress. Culturgeschichte: Die bildenden Künste und das Kunstgewerbe, Theater, Musik, in der Zeit von 1800 bis 1825*, ed. Eduard Leisching (Vienna: Verlag von Arteria & Co., 1898), a profusely illustrated quarto volume, to which one of the contributors was Alois Riegl, published in conjunction with an 1896 exhibition at the K.K. Österreichisches Museum. Very occasionally, the primary object of the publication is announced as artistic rather than historical; thus Auguste de Chambrune in the Foreword to his *Napoléon et ses contemporains. Suite de gravures représentant des traits d'héroïsme, de clémence, de générosité, de popularité, avec texte* (Paris: Jules Renouard, 1828): "Lorsque nous conçûmes le plan de cet ouvrage, notre première idée fut d'élever un monument qui pût attester aux nations étrangères la supériorité de notre école de gravure et assurer à chacun de nos artistes le degré de renommée qu'il mérite pour son talent." (p. v) While this "première idée" was modified later and became one of demonstrating the humanity of Napoléon, Chambrune disclaimed any narrative intent: "Nous n'avons pas la prétention d'écrire l'histoire." (p. xiii)

themselves as testimony to the past was an important contribution to historiography. When the publisher of a new edition of a classic historian such as
Michelet at the turn of the century added portraits by artists contemporary
with their subjects to the text, the style of the portrait was intended to inform
the reader no less than what the portrait represented. Dayot, moreover,
though perhaps more explicit than others about his aims and methods, was
not a unique or completely isolated figure. While Craik and Knight had not
highlighted the expressive, as distinct from representational function of their
illustrations, they had provided material capable of being interpreted as
direct testimony to a culture and way of looking at the world. Besides, more
and more historians active around the same time as Dayot, particularly those
drawn to cultural history, chose to enhance their work with images from the
time they were writing about—ever more faithful reproductions of manuscript illuminations, old oil paintings and portraits, old engravings, contemporary documents and letters, and for more recent times newspaper or
pamphlet pages and photographs. The function of those images was
increasingly expressive as well as representational. Beginning in the 1890s,
editions of J. R. Green's previously unillustrated *Short History of the English
People* (first ed. 1876) included a number of such images [figs. 282, 283]. As
Alice Green, Green's widow, wrote in her preface to an 1895 illustrated edition, it had been "a favourite wish of my husband's to see English History
interpreted and illustrated by pictures which should tell us how men and
things appeared to the lookers-on of their own day, and how contemporary
observers aimed at representing them." The selection of illustrations for new
editions of the *Short History* "therefore has always been determined by a
desire to get at the contemporary view of men and things. [. . .] Indirectly
therefore the whole series of illustrations comes to be an interesting record
not only of the changes that passed over English life, but of some of the
changes that passed over its modes of expression."[167] Likewise, a six-volume
edition (London: Macmillan, 1913–15) of Macaulay's *History of England
from the Accession of James II* prepared by the Regius Professor of History at
Oxford, Charles Harding Firth, was richly illustrated with images from the
appropriate time as were the first five volumes (published in ten) of one of
the most successful of early twentieth-century works of history, the multi-
volume *Histoire de France illustrée* (Paris: Hachette, 1901–11) under the
general editorship of Ernest Lavisse, to which nearly all the leading historians of France at the time contributed.

In Germany, most of the illustrated histories of the last years of the nineteenth century and the early years of the twentieth used images for expressive as well as representational ends. Thus the various individual works
comprising the *Allgemeine Geschichte in Einzeldarstellungen*, a series edited
by Wilhelm Oncken (Berlin: G. Grote 1881), were illustrated by portraits,

---

[167]J.R. Green, *A Short History of the English People* (New York: Harper and Brothers, 1895),
vol. I, pp. v, vii. See also note 111 above on Charlotte M. Waters' 1926 *Economic History of
England 1066-1874*. The retired school headmistress appears to have taken Mrs. Green's
words to heart.

documents, sculpture, architecture, and engravings of scenes dating from the time of the subject matter and intended to communicate in themselves the "spirit of the age" that produced them, as were the two-volume *Deutsche Geschichte*, edited by Ludwig Stacke (Bielefeld and Leipzig: Velhagen & Klasing, 1892) [figs. 284–288], Bernhard Erdmannsdörffer's two-volume *Deutsche Geschichte vom Westfälischen Frieden bis zum Regierungsantritt*

⋙⋙⋙⋙⋙⋙   Der Südosten.   ⋘⋘⋘⋘⋘⋘⋘

Übergabe, doch vertragswidrig wüteten seine Truppen unter den abziehenden Haufen. Die Württemberger sprengte das Heer des Schwäbischen Bundes bei Sindelfingen südwestlich von Stuttgart aus einander, es nahm am 16. Mai Weinsberg und vereinigte sich dann mit den Truppen Ludwigs V. von der Pfalz, der inzwischen die Bauern des Bruchrains zur Übergabe gebracht hatte; mit 2500 Reitern und 8000 Fußknechten rückten die Fürsten dann zum Entsatze der Marienburg vor. Diese hatten am 15. Mai die Belagerer in einem gewaltigen nächtlichen Sturmangriff noch einmal vergeblich zu bezwingen versucht; dann zog auf die Kunde von Sindelfingen zuerst der „helle Haufe" nach Süden ab, stieß aber schon am 2. Juni an der Tauber bei Königshofen auf das fürstliche Heer und löste sich hier, durch Berlichingens heimliche Entfernung

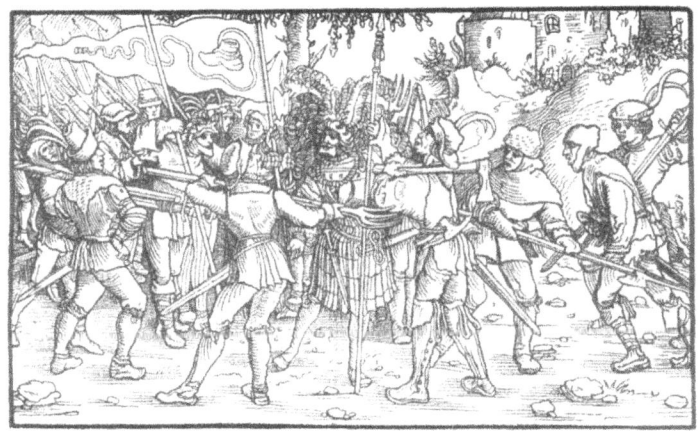

204. Ermordung eines Ritters durch aufrührerische Bauern.
Nach einem Holzschnitt Schäuffelins im „Troſtſpiegel".

entmutigt, ohne eigentlichen Kampf in voller Verwirrung auf; am 1. Juni erlag nach tapferer Gegenwehr der „schwarze Haufe" bei Ingolstadt und Sulz-   1525. dorf, und Florian Geyer starb einen ehrlichen Reitertod. Nun unterwarfen sich rasch Würzburg, Rothenburg und Frankfurt, die Bauern von Mainz und Bamberg, schließlich auch die im Allgäu und im Schwarzwald. Wo nicht Verträge gelangen, was übrigens häufig der Fall war, nicht selten unter Vermittlung der Reichsgewalt, da wüteten erbarmungslose Strafgerichte.

Ohne unmittelbaren Zusammenhang mit diesen Vorgängen, weil die   Der Südosten. bayerischen Herzöge die Lechgrenze militärisch besetzten und jede Regung im Innern mit eiserner Hand niederhielten, spielten sich ähnliche Ereignisse in den Ostalpen und in Tirol ab. Im Salzburgischen, wo die Bergleute den Kern der Bewegungspartei bildeten, wurde der Erzbischof auf seiner Hohensalz- burg belagert, dann erhob sich auch das steirische Ennstal; hier wurde am 2. Juli

FIGURE XXVII Otto Kaemmel, *Deutsche Geschichte* (Leipzig: Otto Spamer, 1911; first ed. 1889), p. 677. Princeton University Library.

Friedrichs des Grossen 1648–1740 (Berlin: G. Grote, 1892-93), and *Spamer's Illustrierte Weltgeschichte mit besonderer Berücksichtigung der Kulturgeschichte* [*Illustrated Universal History with Special Consideration of Cultural History*] in nine volumes, edited by Otto Kaemmel (Leipzig: Otto Spamer,1893–98) [figs. XXVII, XXVIII]. A reproduction of a painting by Jacques-François-Joseph Schwebach representing the Battle of Mount Tabor, for instance, is no longer intended simply to evoke the reality of the battle in the reader's imagination, as in earlier histories, but to convey how an artist who was a contemporary of Napoleon and Kleber painted battle scenes and how contemporary viewers of the painting or print were encouraged to imagine them [figs. 289, 290]. The Lamprecht controversy in the late 1880s having shaken the dominance of what J.R. Green famously described as "drum and trumpet history," illustrations were increasingly expected to show what people in the past wore, what tools they used, what kinds of dwellings they inhabited, what crops they cultivated, but also what they believed and how they saw and felt about their world. Ferdinand Helmolt's *Weltgeschichte* (Leipzig: Bibliographisches Institut, 1899–1907; eight-volume English translation:*The World's History* [London: W. Heinemann, 1901–07]), the first volumes of which were devoted to Asia, Africa, and pre-Columbian America, contained almost exclusively high quality images of archaeological items, of

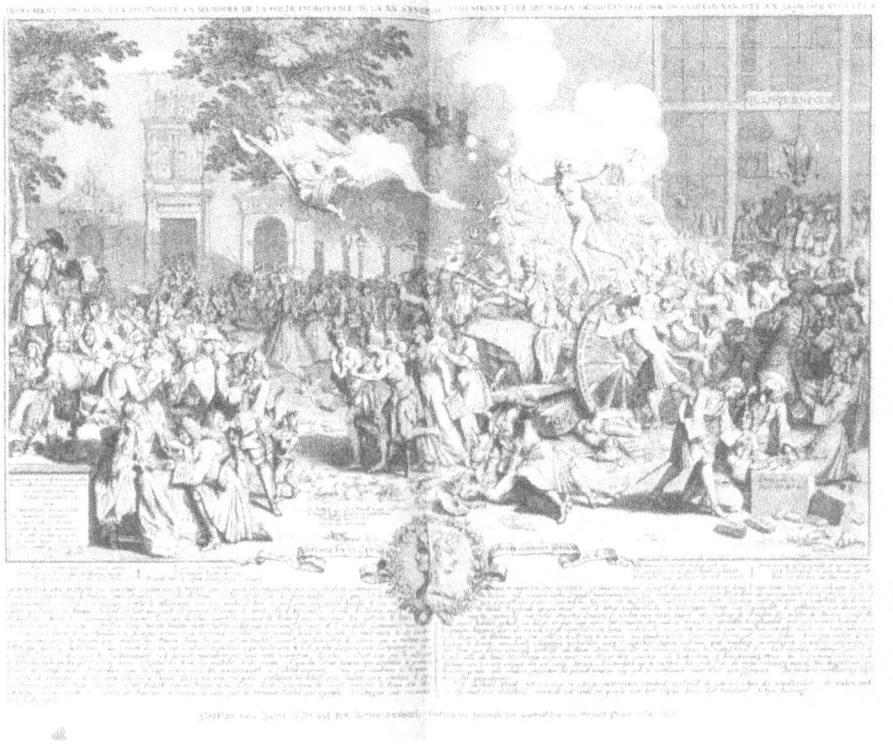

FIGURE XXVIII Bernhard Erdmannsdörffer, *Deutsche Geschichte vom Westfälischen Frieden bis zum Regierungsantritt Friedrichs des Grossen 1648-1740*, 2 vols. (Berlin: G. Grote, 1892-93), vol. 2, between pp. 352 and 353. Princeton University Library.

architecture, and of important documents, and reproductions of old paintings or manuscript illuminations contemporary with their subjects[168] [figs. 291–293]. Eduard Heyck's *Deutsche Geschichte: Volk, Staat, Kultur und geistiges Leben*, published in 1905 by the firm of Velhagen & Klasing (Bielefeld and Leipzig) was similarly illustrated, with "11 Abbildungen in Farbendruck, 277 Abbildungen im Text und 5 Karten" (11 color illustrations, 277 illustrations in the text, and 5 maps) [fig. 294] in the first of its three volumes. Velhagen & Klasing specialized in high-minded, relatively inexpensive educational series for the general public, such as "Künstlermonographien" and "Monographien zur Weltgeschichte," to which many purchasers took out subscriptions. The volume on Bismarck, which Heyck contributed to the latter series (vol. IV, 1898), was enhanced by 190 images from the time. So too, Hans Blum's *Die deutsche Revolution 1848–49*, published by the avant-garde house of Eugen Diederichs to mark the fiftieth anniversary of the 1848 Revolution, contained many illustrations and foldout replicas of flyers and pamphlets from the time.

---

[168]On Helmolt's work, his relation to the father of anthropogeography, Friedrich Ratzel, and an indirect relation to Marc Bloch, see Matthias Middell, "Histoire culturelle, histoire globale, transfert culturel," *Revue Germanique Internationale*, 21 (2004): 227–44.

Epilogue

While many, perhaps most, scholarly history books are still published today without illustrations, wherever illustrations have been used, they have invariably been, for almost a century now, of the kind preferred by Dayot, Green, and Oncken. They may be reproductions of manuscript miniatures, paintings, drawings, lithographs, posters, pages from a manuscript or document, or photographs; what is reproduced is always a product of the age that the reproduction is intended to illustrate. And while they doubtless enhance the appeal to the general reader of the works in which they are employed, these images are no longer predominantly a feature of popular histories. On the contrary, they are now seen as serving a scholarly purpose alongside the charts and graphs that were admitted into the historiographical text around the same time they were. Their purpose is to contribute to the historian's argument by conveying directly, in themselves, the feelings and outlook—the *mentalité*—of the time the historian is writing about. By dispensing with the mediation of a modern artist-illustrator, history thus got to show, as it were, the true face of the past. The image functions in this respect in a similar way to the language or handwriting of documents (a form of illustration especially favored by Dayot and by German historians), inasmuch as the language or handwriting itself conveys information independently of the content of the message. While the statistical graphic, one might say, aims to bring out certain objective structural features that the historian believes are essential to the understanding of the segment of the past he or she is studying or to the argument he or she is making, the function of the image is to bring before our eyes some features of its subjective experience and view of the world. Material history and "histoire des mentalités" are thus joined together no less than "longue durée," "conjoncture," and "événement."

As an example of the changes that have occurred in the last century in the visualizing or figuring of history, we might consider one of the classics of modern historiography, Fernand Braudel's *La Méditerranée et le monde méditerranéen à l'époque de Philippe II*. By synthesizing three historiographical perspectives—"histoire structurale" or history of *la longue durée* (an almost motionless history, close to geography, meteorology, and anthropology), "histoire conjoncturelle" (the history of trends brought on by deep underlying shifts of an economic, demographic, or meteorological nature), and "histoire événémentielle" (the story of individual decisions and actions, close to traditional history)—this great work, ranging as it does well beyond the fields of specialized economic and demographic history, immediately won the respect and admiration of historians of all stripes.[169] Whether because the cost of charts and illustrations would have been prohibitive in the difficult years immediately following World War II, or because the author had not at first envisaged including any, the first edition (Paris: Armand Colin, 1949), in one volume of over one thousand pages, contained no charts or illustrations whatsoever and only two or three small tables.[170] However, by the time of the second edition (1966)—"revue et corrigée" and expanded to two volumes—the book was full of both modern graphs and images from the period covered by the study [figs. XXIX, XXX, 295–300]. Braudel's subsequent works followed the pattern of this second edition. Volume I alone of *Civilisation matérielle et capitalisme (XVe–XVIIIe siècle)* (Paris: Armand Colin, 1967) contains 8 colored plates, 40 black and white plates, 124 smaller images embedded in the text, 9 maps and 9 charts. A later edition of 1979 is even more profusely illustrated [figs. XXIX, XXX, 301–304].

To sum up, the shift in modern historiography, from the investigation and narration of particular events involving particular individual actors in the past to the investigation and exposition of impersonal forces and trends,[171] has finally won a secure place for statistical graphs in historical texts. Graphs are now found not only in highly technical studies, such as those of Labrousse or Chaunu, where they serve to sum up and present clearly and in immediately perceptible, quantitative form a significant trend or relation derived from masses of laboriously collected and painstakingly analyzed data. They also figure in many works intended for and marketed to a larger public, such as Philippe Ariès's *Centuries of Childhood* (New York: Alfed A. Knopf, 1962; orig. French, Paris: Plon, 1960) and *Histoire des populations françaises et de leurs attitudes devant la vie depuis le XVIIIème siècle* (Paris: Editions Self, 1948, reissued by Editions du Seuil, 1971), *L'Invention de la France* by Hervé Le Bras and Emmanuel Todd in the inexpensive Livre de Poche series (Paris, 1981), E.J. Hobsbawm's *Industry and Empire. An Economic History of Britain from 1750 to the Present Day* (first published by Weidenfeld and Nicholson in 1968, reissued a year later as a volume in the Pelican Economic History of Britain series by the mass-market publisher Penguin Books), and the engagingly written, beautifully illustrated, yet rigor-

---

[169]In his preface (dated "Mai, 1946") to the 1949 edition, Braudel also uses two other sets of terms to describe this tripartite division: "histoire quasi immobile," "histoire lentement rythmée" "histoire traditionnelle" and "temps géographique," "temps social," "temps individuel." On Braudel's classic work and its reception, see Peter Burke, *The French Historical Revolution: The "Annales" School*, ch. 3, "The Age of Braudel."

[170]One of these tables shows the prices of wheat from the North at Livorno in 1593; another shows journey times, outgoing and return, between Venice and various Eastern Mediterranean ports used by pilgrims to the Holy Land.

[171]Alain Corbin, Robert Darnton, and Natalie Davis explore individual, even exceptional cases, but still with a view to a deeper, more nuanced understanding, through them, of the larger picture.

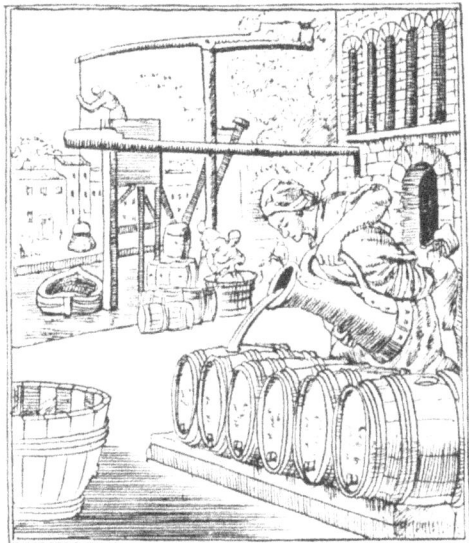

Fig. 46. Le transport de la bière (1699). On remplit les tonneaux et on les charge dans une barque, à l'aide d'une grue rudimentaire, à contrepoids et pivotante. (*D'après* une gravure de C. Luyken.)

FIGURE XXIX Fernand Braudel, *Civilisation matérielle et capitalisme (XVe–XVIIIe siècle)* (Paris: Armand Colin, 1967), p. 179. By kind permission of the publisher.

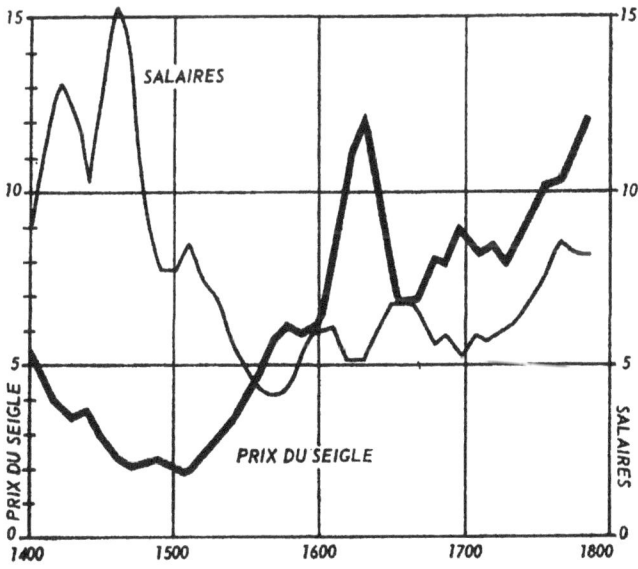

Graphique 7. Salaires et prix du seigle à Gœttingen (XV°-XIX° siècle). Le prix du seigle est calculé en *reichmark* d'argent et le salaire (qui est celui d'un bûcheron travaillant à façon) est exprimé en kilogrammes de seigle. La corrélation est évidente entre montée des prix du seigle et baisse du salaire réel, et réciproquement. (*D'après* W. Abel.)

FIGURE XXX Fernand Braudel, *Civilisation matérielle et capitalisme (XVe–XVIIIe siècle)* (Paris: Armand Colin, 1967), p. 101. By kind permission of the publisher.

ously scholarly books of Lawrence Stone: *Crisis of the Aristocracy 1558–1641* (Oxford: Clarendon Press, 1965; over 20 graphs), *The Family, Sex, and Marriage in England 1500–1800* (New York: Harper and Row, 1977; 16 graphs), *An Open Elite? England 1540–1880* (Oxford: Clarendon Press, 1984; over 50 graphs), and *Road to Divorce: England 1530–1987* (Oxford: Oxford University Press, 1990; over 30 graphs) [figs. 305–310]. Not least important, graphs have been widely adopted in history textbooks for schools, to which the advantage claimed for them by their eighteenth-century inventor—the ability to "facilitate the attainment of information, and aid the memory in retaining it"—makes them especially suited[172] [figs. 311–315]. At the same time traditional illustration has undergone a thorough transformation as its function has come to be archaeological and anthropological rather than dramatic—that of evoking the sensibilites, worldviews, and material conditions of past communities and cultures rather than representing particular moments in a narrative. Even when photographs are used to illustrate specific persons or events, they function partly as testimony in themselves to past ways of looking at the world, and not simply as pictorial re-presentations [figs. 316, 317]. A new vision of history has led inevitably to new ways of figuring history.

---

[172]E.g., R.R. Sellman, *A Practical Guide to Modern British Economic History from 1700 to the Present Day* (London: E. Arnold, 1947), "intended primarily for pupils taking Economic History as part of their School Certificate Course, but [. . .] also suitable for third year forms in secondary schools" (Foreword); J.L. Gayler, Irene Richards, J.A. Morris, *A Sketch-Map Economic History of Britain* (London: Harrap, 1957)—"intended for students taking the GCE [General Certificate of Education] exams"; John and Gweneth Stokes, *Europe and the Modern World 1870-1970* (London: Longman, 1973); Jean Guiffan, Victor Prévot, Anne-Marie Siflet, *Histoire du monde moderne* (Paris: Librairie classique Eugène Belin, 1974)—a textbook for the use of students in 2ème (the penultimate class in the French lycée).

www.ingramcontent.com/pod-product-compliance
Lightning Source LLC
Chambersburg PA
CBHW080422190526
45161CB00004B/256

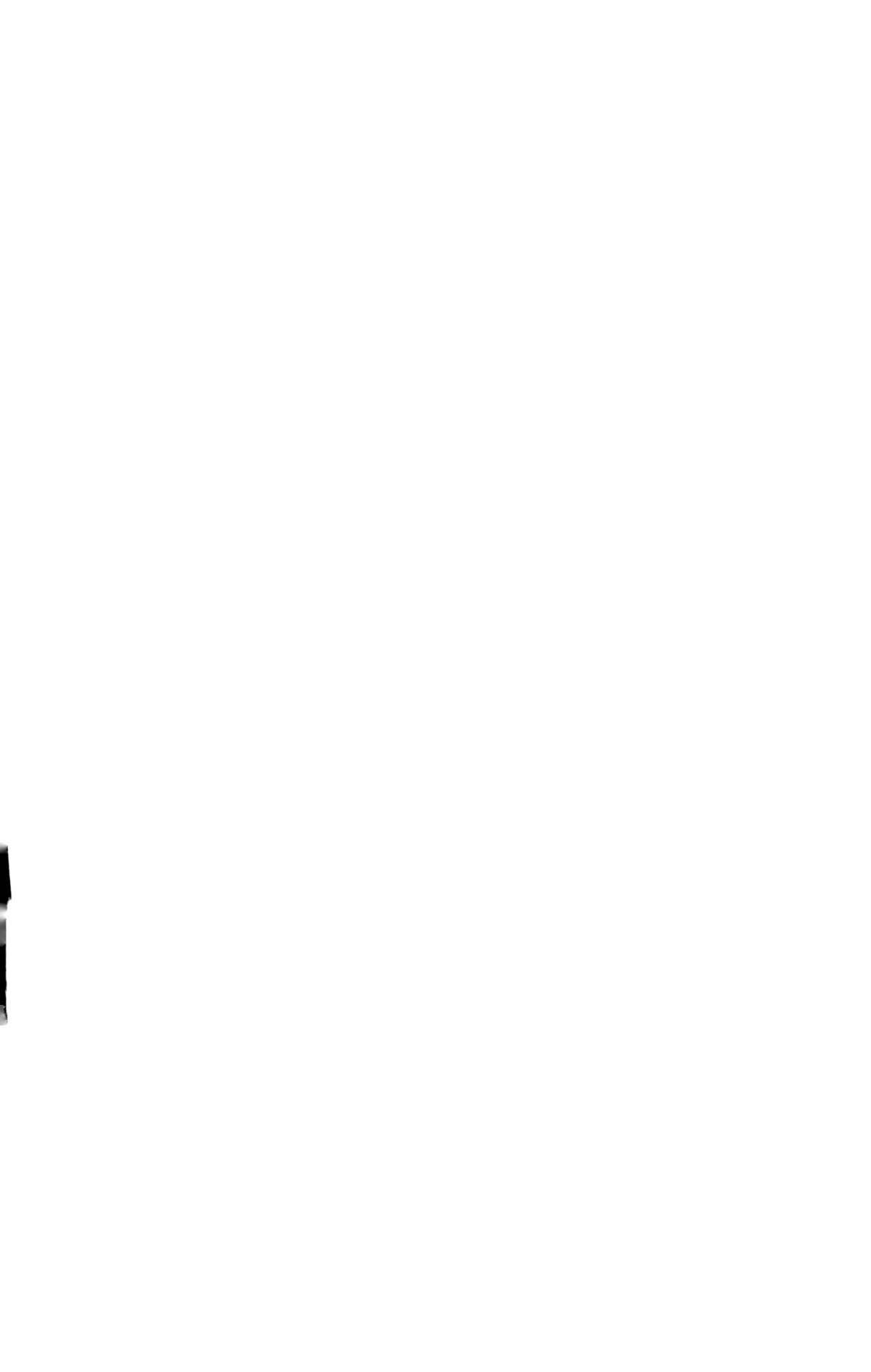